FROM FRUSTRATION TO FREEDOM

From Frustration to Freedom

KAREN DOCKREY

VICTOR BOOKS
A DIVISION OF SCRIPTURE PRESS PUBLICATIONS INC.
USA CANADA ENGLAND

Background reading sources used in the writing of this study include:

Barrett, C.K. *The Epistle to the Romans* (New York: Harper and Row, 1957).
Cranfield, C.E.B. *Romans* (Edinburgh, T & T. Clark, 1975).
Jenkins, David. "Youth in Discovery" Bible Commentary in Curriculum Unit on Spiritual Gifts. (Nashville: Convention Press, 1991).
MacGorman, J.W. "Romans," "1 Corinthians," in the Layman's Bible Commentary Series (Nashville: Broadman Press, 1980).
Newman, B.M. and Nida, E.A. *A Translator's Handbook on Paul's Letter to the Romans* (New York: United Bible Societies, 1973).
Ridenour, Fritz. *How to Be a Christian Without Being Religious* (Ventura, Calif.: Gospel Light, 1967).
Notes from:
   Good News Bible
   New International Version Study Bible
   New International Version Student Bible
   Oxford Annotated Bible

Scripture quotations are from the *Holy Bible, New International Version,* © 1973, 1978, 1984, International Bible Society. Used by permission of Zondervan Bible Publishers.

Copyediting: LaMoyne Schneider
Cover Design: Larry Taylor
Cover Illustration: Joe Van Severen

Recommended Dewey Decimal Classification: 227.1
Suggested Subject Heading: BIBLE, N.T., ROMANS

ISBN: 0-89693-233-8

1   2   3   4   5   6   7   8   9   10   Printing/Year   96   95   94   93   92

VICTOR BOOKS
A division of SP Publications, Inc.
Wheaton, Illinois 60187

CONTENTS

The presence of pain and struggle doesn't mean your faith is inferior or that you lack faith. Pain and struggle are part of living on earth. They compel you to seek the cause of the problem, address it with God's help, and move toward freedom in Christ. Struggles can motivate you to escape from meaninglessness to purpose, from frustration to freedom.

This Bible study, based on passages in Romans, will guide you to discover how God can equip you to find freedom in Christ in the midst of trials. As you study Romans, talk with God and with other Christians about the struggles you have with hypocrisy, pride, suffering, bad habits, sin, sadness, anger, loneliness, and feeling useless. Rather than seek simplistic answers, search God's Word for principles that apply to your specific situations.

The Book of Romans is excellent for resolving struggles because it is a treatise on the meaning of life. It speaks to the battles faced by Christians and non-Christians alike. It also demonstrates how and why God triumphs, even in complicated situations. The first several chapters address truths about God (theology), while the last several chapters explain how to live according to those truths (ethics). As you study the early chapters, continually ask yourself, *What difference does this truth make in my life?* As you study later chapters, ask yourself, *What truths about God form the reason for this command or guideline?*

The day-to-day living out of our faith is the target of this study guide. As we let Jesus guide and empower our lives, we find peace, solutions, strength, and power. He impacts every area of life and enables us to move from struggle to security. This freedom is not spontaneous but happens as we deliberately make decisions to obey God and live His way.

Romans is the longest, most carefully composed of Paul's letters, and perhaps the most influential. Such persons as Augustine, Martin Luther, and John Wesley experienced spiritual renewal by reading Romans. Let spiritual renewal begin within you too as you study these passages.

Paul, formerly called Saul, had been dramatically converted from Judaism to Christianity on his way to persecute Christians (see Acts 9:1-

31). Having been a vehemently committed Jew, he became an even more firmly committed Christian.

At the time, Rome was the undisputed center of power, civilization, and learning. The Romans to whom Paul wrote were a sophisticated audience with big demands and important questions. Paul's letter addressed them brilliantly and precisely. Paul began the church in Rome; but, at the time he wrote, he hadn't personally visited the believers there.

Evidence indicates that Paul wrote Romans sometime between A.D. 54 and 58. He had been collecting funds from churches in Greece and Asia Minor for the needy Jerusalem church. Paul wrote the letter to the Romans while waiting to deliver this collection. He hoped to visit the Romans afterward (see Rom. 15:28).

Inspired by God, Paul carefully summarized massive spiritual truths in the 16 chapters of Romans. The book examines why all people need to be reconciled to God and why living God's way brings joy. Romans 1:16-17 summarizes the theme of the letter:

> I am not ashamed of the Gospel, because it is the power of God for the salvation of everyone who believes: first for the Jew, then for the Gentile. For in the Gospel a righteousness from God is revealed, a righteousness that is by faith from first to last, just as it is written: "The righteous will live by faith."

Working through the Study
Each session in this guide has four components: inductive study questions (*Listen to God's Word*) to walk you through the Scriptures; a narrative section (*Life Example*) sharing one person's understanding of how to live the passage being studied; exercises and challenges designed to help you apply Bible truths to your daily life (*Live God's Word*); and a leader's guide to aid in group study.

For each study, you will need a Bible, this study guide, plus any other materials named by the leader (if you have one). You may want a notebook to record journal entries and discoveries from your personal study and group meetings. You could also use it to list prayer requests in a group setting plus their resolutions.

If you are studying on your own, make a point of sharing what you are learning with someone else. You will solidify lessons in your mind while you bless your friend.

If you are part of a group, you will find it most helpful to work through the study questions on your own before the group meets. Then you will be ready to share what you learned from the passage and how it applies to your life, plus any questions that arose as you studied. Members will profit from hearing one another's insights and perceptions.

Whether you study alone or lead a group, you may choose those questions or exercises that fit your needs or your group's.

Using the study questions, work through the Scripture passage *before* you read the narrative section; in this way, your initial findings will all be original.

Throughout the study, remember that the Holy Spirit is your teacher. Ask Him to give you eyes to see His truth and a heart ready to obey it.

As you come across questions that call for you to connect the truth of the passage to your own life, answer them prayerfully. Let the Spirit guide you in applying God's Word to your life. When you find something in the passage that makes you feel grateful to God, thank Him! When something leads you to praise Him, stop and do so! When the Spirit points to something in your life that doesn't measure up to what you're reading in Scripture, let Him speak to you. Confess any sin and allow God to cleanse you and lead you in the right direction.

CHAPTER ONE

FROM BELIEF TO

❧ *LISTEN TO GOD'S WORD* ❧

It doesn't matter what you believe as long as you're sincere.
That's fine for you, but it just doesn't work for me.

These well-meaning but totally erroneous statements fail to make the connection between belief and reality. Likewise, no matter how strongly I believe I can fly by flapping my arms, I can't. And no matter how strongly I believe the sun revolves around the earth, it doesn't. Beliefs are not meant to be icing-on-the-cake philosophies having little to do with everyday life. They do, however, impact our actions and make a difference in how we approach life's challenges. Beliefs should not be formed by choosing how we want to perceive reality. Rather, they must result from discovering how things are in this life and in the hereafter. Then we follow our beliefs by shaping our lives around reality.

Our beliefs about Jesus Christ can totally change our lives. For this reason, take in God's revelation as you study Romans 1:16-32. Notice that faith, or lack of it, has power to impact your daily living.

Read Romans 1:16-32.
  1. Romans 1:16-17 summarizes Paul's theme for the Book of Romans. How would you describe the Gospel? How does Paul do so?

How do the Gospel's "power . . . for salvation" and "righteousness from God" give you power and rightness in your daily life?

11

2. The last part of verse 17 is a quote from Habakkuk 2:4. Read Habakkuk 1:1–2:4 and 3:17-19. How is faith both trust and action?

3. Every person makes a decision to accept or reject God. What about those who have never heard of God? Can they know or accept Him? How? (See Rom. 1:18-20.) Are they accountable for their actions? Why?

4. God's wrath (see 1:18) is not an angry attack. Instead, God's wrath is seen in His refusal to protect us from the consequences of our actions. The phrase "God gave them over" (vv. 24, 26, 28) shows this wrath. What consequences did people create for themselves in each instance?

Verses 24-25:

Verses 26-27:

Verses 28-32:

Why is this expression of God's wrath more effective than His inflicting punishment or striking us with lightning?

5. Every person can know about God because He teaches everybody about Himself through what He has made. What do the following elements of God's created world teach you about Him? (See v. 20.)

People (each individual's uniqueness, creativity):

Earth (nature, water, land):

Seasons (predictability, variety, beauty):

Solar system (orderliness, vast dimensions):

Time (forwardness, steadiness, longness/shortness):

Other:

6. People can respond to God in two ways: by accepting Him or rejecting Him. Both choices are revealed in action. Why do you think people ignore God, even when they know about Him and know the consequences of disobeying Him? (See vv. 21-23, 32.)

Ignoring God sounds like something that gives people freedom. Why does it actually take freedom from them? (See vv. 21-32.)

7. People reject God in several basic ways. Name examples of these ways from your experience and from Romans 1:21-32.

Arrogance (vv. 21-22, 28):

Idolatry (vv. 21, 23-25):

Relationship distortion (vv. 26-27):

Cruelty (vv. 28-32):

How does refusing to glorify God or give thanks to God lead to each sin?

8. People need to worship. If they choose not to worship God, they end up worshiping someone or something else. Arrogance is a brand of self-worship. Idolatry involves worship of things or people. Why are self, things, and people poor worship substitutes for God? (See vv. 21-23, 25.)

Putting self, things, or people in God's place causes most of the problems in our world. Give several examples.

9. Sex is designed to express an intimate human relationship. How does refusing to be intimate with God affect sexual intimacy? (See vv. 24, 26-27.)

Read Leviticus 18:22 and reread Romans 1:24, 26-27. Why is homosexuality a destructive lifestyle choice rather than an alternative lifestyle choice?

10. "Knowledge of God" is not mere head knowledge but taking Him into account in everyday decisions and actions. Why does ignoring God confuse thinking? (See v. 28.)

Confused thinking leads to destructive living. Which of the vices in verses 29-31 are you prone to? What damage do these actions cause?

11. What is wrong with approving of those who practice wickedness? (See v. 32.) How does it increase sin?

How is approval a suppression of the truth? (See v. 18.)

12. What would you say to someone who said, "I'm a basically good person. I mind my own business and don't hurt anyone. Therefore, I don't need God in my life"?

13. This passage is full of examples of how to show you do not believe in God. Reread the passage, citing a positive example for each negative one. How would these positive actions or attitudes show you do believe God?

For Further Study
Romans is an overview of the meaning of life with Christ. Write what you think life in Christ means. Then read Romans 1–16. Expand your explanation based on your reading discoveries.

LIFE EXAMPLE:
❧ Let Every Action Honor God ❧

"Are homosexuals going to hell? The Bible says that, doesn't it?" asked Julia, a new Christian trying to make sense of all she had learned about faith and practice. She was thinking of 1 Corinthians 6:9-10, which lists several types of sinners who will not inherit the kingdom of God—the wicked, sexually immoral, idolaters, adulterers, male prostitutes, homosexual offenders, thieves, the greedy, drunkards, slanderers, and swindlers. These people can't become part of the kingdom because they work in direct opposition to God. They demonstrate by their behavior that God and His teachings matter little, if at all, to them.

God distinguishes these offenders by their practices but not by their value. He wants to redeem homosexuals, prostitutes, and the greedy just as much as those who have been "good" all their lives. According to 1 Corinthians 6:11, Jesus Christ washes, sanctifies, and justifies (declares right with Himself) each person who turns to Him. A relationship with Jesus Christ—not past performance—is the key to going to heaven.

Homosexuality is wrong, not because people deem it so, but because it alters God's good plan for love and relationships. Two bodies of the same sex are not meant to fit together in sexual union. A same-sex marriage cannot produce children. A homosexual relationship lacks the richness of maleness and femaleness together.

Two persons of the same sex can be attracted to each other, but that attraction is, at best, friendship. True, some same-sex relationships last longer and are more caring than some heterosexual ones, but physical union and marriage are not to be part of these relationships.

Those who teach that homosexuality is a viable alternative lifestyle sincerely believe this is true. They even have statistics to verify the numbers born with a homosexual orientation. But sincerity and practice don't validate rightness. Not all natural tendencies are good ones. Fulfilling homosexual desires is similar to saying, "I have a predisposition toward stealing. I feel drawn toward it and I don't feel guilty when I do it. So it is right for me." No matter how strong, homosexual urges must not be expressed any more than thieving urges must be expressed.

Homosexual yearnings do exist, but their existence doesn't confirm their rightness. When persons feel romantically inclined toward the same sex, it's a problem, not a gift. These persons need help, not encouragement. Like the rest of us sinners, they need compassion, not rejection. They need strategies for redirecting homosexual feelings, just as shoplifters need strategies to motivate them to pay rather than pilfer. The issue is not an easy one, nor will it be solved overnight. But as we let God empower us, we become wise enough to handle it.

Homosexuality is not "somebody else's" problem. It's a part of our problem, the sin problem. Lest you become smug and decide that you are safe in your heterosexual orientation, notice the other actions in the Romans' and 1 Corinthians' lists. *Homosexual offenders* produce pain and confusion just as *slander* leads to division and bickering. Homosexual expression is sin, but no worse sin than boasting, greed, strife, deceit, malice, gossip, arrogance, or worshiping created things. Homosexual expression is no greater sin than deceiving your heterosexual mate. Which sin traps are you most likely to fall into? What misconceptions lead you to them?

"I'm not greedy—I deserve nice things."

"She is impossible to get along with, so it's OK to ignore her."

"I can't tell the truth or it would hurt their feelings."

"So what if it hurts her—it's true!"

Practicing homosexuals have let false beliefs lead to false actions. When have you done the same? False beliefs and the sins that follow them are serious, no matter what the offense.

Romans 1:16-32 explains that we must act on what we know about God. Working against God's revelations, whether intentionally or not, causes agony for us and those around us. When a belief is wrong, wrong behavior follows. Ignoring God or believing incorrectly about Him leads to distorted actions. Notice how Romans 1 underscores this:

☐ "[They] suppress the truth by their wickedness" (v. 18).
☐ "Their thinking became futile and their foolish hearts were darkened" (v. 21).
☐ "God gave them over in the sinful desires of their hearts" (v. 24).
☐ "[They] received in themselves the due penalty for their perversion" (v. 27).
☐ "He gave them over to a depraved mind, to do what ought not to be done" (v. 28).
☐ "They have become filled with every kind of wickedness, evil,

greed, and depravity. . . . envy, murder, strife, deceit, and malice. They are gossips, slanderers, God-haters, insolent, arrogant, and boastful" (vv. 29-30).

☐ "They invent ways of doing evil" (v. 30).

☐ "They are senseless, faithless, heartless, ruthless" (v. 31).

☐ "Although they know . . . those who do such things deserve death, they not only continue to do these very things but also approve of those who practice them" (v. 32).

Notice that all persons have the same choice—to believe God for who He is, or to make Him into the image they want. Homosexuality is a visible sin, but just as damaging are the more "acceptable" sins, such as the strife and slander within heterosexual marriage. Your devotion to Christ affects every relationship you influence, every commitment you make, every action you take. Choose to know God and to glorify Him with every word, action, and attitude.

🕊 LIVE GOD'S WORD 🕊

1. As you studied Romans 1:16-32, you may have thought of persons or groups of persons you believe are guilty of the sins named. Refuse, though, to focus on others; examine your own life. When are you most likely to ignore God? What sins result from this? Write your insights in a journal. Let your writings be a conversation with God.
2. Memorize Romans 1:20 while sitting outside. During the day, note the ways God teaches you about Himself through people, nature, and animals. At night, note how He does this through the majesty of the universe.
3. Ponder God's expectations of you. Why does He expect you to understand Him? To obey Him? To glorify and thank Him? To heed Him in everyday decisions and actions?
4. Pinpoint a problem in your life. Trace it back to a point where you or someone else ignored God. Decide how glorifying God, giving thanks to Him, affirming His truth, and obeying Him can correct this problem or make it easier to cope with. Then do these very things.
5. Write a letter to someone you know (or hope to meet) who may know God through creation (see vv. 18-20) but has never heard or understood the Gospel of Jesus Christ (see vv. 16-17). Explain the Gospel in words he or she would understand.

CHAPTER TWO

FROM HYPOCRISY TO

❧ *LISTEN TO GOD'S WORD* ❧

"I don't see how Zoe can call herself a Christian. She is such a gossip. She's always talking about people at church. Instead of waiting to see if the things she repeats are true, she tells everyone every little thing."

What's wrong with this story? The speaker is gossiping about gossip!

Most of us find it easier to notice the faults in others than to observe and correct our own disobedience. Many of us feel so secure in our identity as Christians that we forget our need to obey daily. Attack these problems head-on by pinpointing areas of hypocrisy in your life and transforming them to integrity. Find freedom from the pressure to judge in Paul's advice to the religious Jews in Romans 2:1-29.

Read Romans 2:1-29.

1. Romans 1 emphasized that ignoring God leads to destructive sins. Reading that chapter may make you feel self-righteous, even judgmental. What's wrong with these attitudes, according to Romans 2:1-3?

2. How is God's judgment different from human judgment? (See vv. 2, 4.)

3. When you want people to "get what they deserve," notice what you deserve for your actions. How will this change your viewpoint? (See v. 4.)

How does God's kindness, tolerance, and patience lead you toward repentance? When does it lead you toward something else?

4. The Jews' rejection of God was cloaked in religious rightness (see v. 5). Similarly, being active in church can make us forget our need for God, His corrections, and His compassions. Why is this "good attitude" dangerous?

Which is easier to correct—blatant or subtle rebellion against God? Of which are you guiltier?

5. On Judgment Day, God "will give to each person according to what he has done" (v. 6). What actions and attitudes will you present to God on that day?

6. Verses 7-8 encourage us to choose actions that produce good. The opposite of this is seeking to please self, regardless of its rightness or its effects on others. Name specific actions that are good and thus seek glory, honor, and immortality in these areas.

Family relationships:

Workplace:

Church service:

Other relationships and commitments:

Is the rightness of an action a stronger motivation to do good, or is the certainty of God's judgment? Why?

7. We obey God because He has saved us, not in order to earn salvation. What's the difference between feeling secure in our salvation and assuming a privileged status with God? (See vv. 9-11.)

8. Verses 9-16 explain that those who have more of God's revelation will be more accountable before Him. Would you rather know the Law and be judged by it, or not know the Law and be judged apart from it? (See vv. 12-16.) Why?

How does learning the Law as revealed in the Bible make it easier to know and obey God?

9. Obedience—not status or Bible knowledge—is the key issue in showing love for God. People raised in church ("Jews"; those "under the Law") as well as those not raised in church ("Gentiles"; "apart from the Law") will face God's judgment. In what ways are you like a Jew? (See vv. 12-13.) A Gentile? (See vv. 14-15.)

Why is action more important than intention or identity? (See vv. 6, 13, 25-29.)

10. Each individual is accountable to God. How reliable is one's conscience as an indicator of God's will? Of right and wrong? (See v. 15.)

11. An accurate judgment of a person is based not on her observable behavior alone but on things that happen between her and God ("secrets," v. 16). Why is God the only one qualified to judge such motives and intentions?

12. The Jews confidently preached the value of God's Law but ignored it themselves. Jot down examples of this from verses 17-24.

Read Matthew 5:21-48 for a clearer understanding of Romans 2:21-24. Which offense do you find most appalling? Which are you most likely to commit?

Why is it easier to advocate loyalty and obedience than to live them?

13. Circumcision is an outward sign of an inward commitment to God. Though also practiced by other cultures, it had a special meaning for Jews: God had assigned it as a sign of covenant (see Gen. 17:9-14). How valuable is circumcision? (See Rom. 2:25-27.)

14. "Circumcision of the heart" (v. 29) is directed and performed by the Holy Spirit (see Deut. 10:16). It is a continuous occurrence rather than a one-time ceremony. How is this operation being performed in you?

15. In verses 28-29, Paul distinguishes between a true Jew and a counterfeit Jew. Is this judging? Why is this distinction permissible?

What is the difference between passing judgment and honestly evaluating another's lifestyle with a goal of helping or discerning?

For Further Study
Recall the heritage of the Jews and how it impacted their understanding of God. As you study, consider Genesis 17; Deuteronomy 6; and Joshua 24. Reflect on your own heritage and how it has given you both accurate and inaccurate understandings of God. Let the Bible correct the inaccuracies.

LIFE EXAMPLE:
🐚 In the Looking Glass 🐚

"He did it again!" I lamented to my weary and ready-for-bed husband. I had returned home from another too-long committee meeting. "After missing last week's meeting, So-and-So proceeded to tell us a long and detailed story about his trip, asked what we were discussing, offered an overly simplistic solution, and then changed the agenda. Just who does he think he is? He is the most selfish person I've ever encountered!"

After several more minutes of agitated spouting, I bid my husband good night. His steady breathing assured me he was sleeping and reminded me of the steadiness of his care. As my mind raced, I recalled the struggles we had walked through together, the victories we celebrated, the little things we cherished, the ways we tolerated each other. He had waited for me once again that morning when I was late.

My rapidly firing brain directed my thoughts down a new track. *I did it again.* After endless promises to be on time, I had been late again. My husband waited patiently but wasn't happy about it. It's not that I want him to get mad or to hold it over my head. What I really want is the motivation and the power to change. Grace—that's what he had shown me: a kindness, tolerance, and patience that made me want to change. He didn't hide his irritation, but underneath it, I knew he cared.

I'm seeing a connection, I thought, as humility seeped through the cracks in the wall of my pride. My tendency to be late is quite convenient for me but keeps my friends waiting, gives my children a hurried start to school, and makes it hard for my husband to count on me. I steal their time just as certainly as my fellow committee member had stolen mine tonight. *"You who preach against stealing, do you steal?"* (Rom. 2:21) God and my husband together wait for me to manage my time in a considerate way. Rather than rant and rave about me, they continue to communicate their expectations, suggest solutions, and continue to care.

My own misbehavior doesn't excuse the actions of my fellow committee member. But my humility can make the problem easier to deal with.

Confronting him would be much more effective with my own shortcomings in mind. The grace I experience makes me more willing to accept that I might not be the best person to point out the problem. God will do so in His own way and with His own messenger. The point is that my antagonist and I both do wrong and are accountable to God, who "will give to each person according to what he has done" (Rom. 2:6).

My fellow committee member and I need neither permission to continue our sin nor judgmental rejection. We need direct but caring honesty, motivation to change, and support while we do so. We need the kind of attitude that sees Christianity as a pilgrimage, a trip in which each step brings us closer to Christlikeness. I become Christlike when I value my friends and family enough to be on time. Still, I must caution myself against judging. Why is my judging dangerous?

- ☐ I am not qualified.
- ☐ I tend to use it to show my superiority.
- ☐ My judgment can be the opposite of kindness, tolerance, and patience.
- ☐ My judgment may be more for my convenience than to draw persons toward repentance.
- ☐ Judgment is God's job.

Refusing to judge means I replace my frustration with positive action.

- ☐ I talk directly to the person with whom I have a problem rather than complain to someone else.
- ☐ I express the same kindness, tolerance, and patience God does toward me.
- ☐ I find ways to deepen Christlike love for persons who offend me, rather than create distance.
- ☐ I work to find actions that solve the problem.
- ☐ I focus on changing my own disobedient actions, the only ones I'm responsible for and the only ones I can change.

The people who motivate me to do good are those who love me as I am, not those who criticize me. The people who enhance me and bring out the good in me are those who talk honestly and humbly with me, not those who judge me. This means I'll get further solving my frustrations by practicing loving honesty than condemning criticism.

Lord Jesus, teach me to love without criticizing. Holy Spirit, circumcise my heart (see Rom. 2:29).

❧ LIVE GOD'S WORD ❧

1. Memorize Romans 2:4. Record in your journal
   □ ways you have been hypocritical;
   □ times you take God's kindness, tolerance, and patience for granted rather than let them lead you to repentance.
   □ areas in which you need to repent and change your actions.
2. Deliberately change an area of your life after repentance. For example:
   STEP 1: Give up gossip for a month. Intentionally close your mouth when tempted to repeat something negative, even if it is true. Remind yourself that God is in the redeeming business and wants to lead the person(s) you gossip about to repentance.
   STEP 2: Develop the habit of repeating good things you hear about people.
   STEP 3: Give up gossip forever.
3. Use three pieces of modeling clay or aluminum foil to create shapes representing God's kindness, tolerance, and patience. Draw or describe them, if you prefer. How does visualizing these characteristics make them more real to you? Thank God for loving you with kindness, tolerance, and patience. Talk with Him about how to show them as you love other people.
4. Find one or more Christian friends to whom you can be accountable. Get in the habit of informing each other when you repent and how you plan to change your actions. Love each other with God's kindness, tolerance, and patience while holding up high standards for each other.

CHAPTER THREE

FROM RELIGION TO

๕ *LISTEN TO GOD'S WORD* ๕

Who do you try to please? Yourself? Your husband? Your church? A friend? God? You can find freedom from the pressure to please. Discover in Romans 3:9–4:25 that faith, not actions done to please God, is the foundation of security in Christ. As you trust Him, you discover that He already loves you. Because He loves you, you are free to express your faith in God-honoring actions.

Read Romans 3:9–4:25.

1. Religion didn't benefit the Jews very much. Why not? (See 3:9-18.)

> If you were raised in the church, you (like the Jews) may find a certain security in that fact. Tell why.

> If you were not raised in the church, you may feel insecure about spiritual things. Tell why.

> Whether you feel secure or insecure, tell why you need Jesus (see vv. 19-20).

2. Christianity is a relationship, not a religion. Write the words and phrases from 3:21-31 which point to that relationship, or which describe God's personal care for you.

How do you feel about God loving you this way?

3. Relationships have more power than religion, but some people feel safer with religion or with what they perceive as goodness. Why?

   What does Romans 3:27-31 say about confidence in religion, also described as observing the Law?

4. Why is God's justice an expression of His love? (See vv. 25-26.)

   Notice the personal relationship between "justice" and "justifies" in verse 26. Comment on it.

5. A relationship with God doesn't mean the Law is no longer important. Rather, your relationship gives you a new reason to obey God. Explain verse 31 in your own words, using the surrounding verses to help you.

6. Abraham, who lived before the giving of the Old Testament law, pleased God the same way God wants us to please Him. Describe Abraham's experience with religion and relationship with God (see 4:1-22).

   Notice the words "believe," "trust," and "faith." What part do they play in a relationship with God? If a passage were written about your relationship with God, how would these words be used?

7. The Jews felt very secure before God because, as physical descendants of Abraham, they had been chosen by God. They felt that circumcision and keeping of the Law enhanced this standing. Discover the facts about this by focusing on some key words in Romans 4:9-17. Jot down the numbers of the verses where "circumcised" and "offspring" appear, plus what you learn from them about the circumcised and the offspring.

Circumcised:

Offspring:

What religious actions or good works in your life could give you reason to think you are righteous? What's wrong with this pride? (See 3:23, 27-28; 4:2, 13-15; also 1 Cor. 1:31.)

8. Churched persons and unchurched persons alike come to God in the same way. How? (See Rom. 4:3-12.)

9. True faith expresses itself in everyday life. Abraham expressed faith in the face of the infertility he and Sarah had (see 4:18-21). Name a situation in your life where you have or could have faith.

Notice that God had promised something specific and Abraham believed Him (see v. 21). Abraham did not tell God what to do. When is your faith a command rather than a response to God? When is your faith a response?

10. Why is faith a relationship word? (See 3:21-22; 4:16-25.)

11. Ultimately, faith is a positive response to God. Faith begins with salvation and continues through obedience (see 4:16; also 10:9-11). Write about your initial positive response to God (when you became a Christian). Or if you have not yet become a Christian, consider making that positive response now by inviting Jesus to be your Savior and Lord. Write your prayer below (see Rom. 10:9-10). Talk to Jesus as to a friend.

Write about how you have responded to God positively today (or yesterday) through obedience.

12. Based on Romans 3–4 and your relationship with God, why is your faith more powerful when expressed through that relationship than when expressed through religion?

For Further Study

God's invitation to salvation has been given through real people in real history. Study the ways this took place by reading Romans 9–10. Notice that a true child of God is one who responds to Him, not merely one who belongs to a specific race or chosen group.

LIFE EXAMPLE:
♣ Love for a Child ♣

No one teaches us more about loving God than our own children. We discover in them the strength of relationship, the value of trust. Words are inadequate to describe the depth of concern good parents feel for their children. We yearn for their happiness and work toward their spiritual, emotional, and physical safety. We protect them with a fierceness that is powerful. We agonize when they hurt, and would give our lives for theirs. Think of your own child(ren)'s individuality, compassion, insight, creativity, eagerness, and thoughtfulness. If you do not have any children in your home, think of a child you know. What would you do to help him or her continue to grow, to love, to learn, to relate, to enjoy?

Perhaps the most amazing part of parenting is the persistence of our love for our children. We may become angry, exhausted, or frustrated, but our love still runs deep. No matter how many times the little ones dirty their diapers, we change them. When they spit up on us, we clean them up first and worry more about their fevers than our smelly clothes. When older ones disobey, we work harder to help them understand what is right. Each smile or hug makes the care-giving more than worthwhile.

Part of parenting is providing security and motivating goodness. When a toddler rushes for the street, we parents yell for her to stop and run to scoop her away from the approaching car. We erect fences to keep her away from future dangers. When she yearns for greater adventure and climbs the fence, we bring her in the house and explain that she cannot go back outside until she stops climbing the fence. She learns to do right because of the consequences of not doing right. She stays out of the street, keeps from hitting playmates, and eats her green beans because of the punishment she receives if she does not obey.

Older children find better motivation for being good. They obey because it brings joy to them and their parents, and ultimately because their behavior brings joy to God. They no longer need fences in the backyard because they understand the danger of traffic. But they need other fences—guidelines for friendships and dating, suggestions for problem-solving, rules against certain activities. These guidelines, suggestions, and rules are designed for their safety, health, and happiness.

Sometimes children try to climb over these fences. Other times they trust us parents. They heed our advice because they love us, not because they'll be punished if they don't. They discover that the rule leads to joy, not away from it.

This trust is precious beyond measure, but it doesn't come automatically. Children will sometimes think their parents want to keep them from having fun. Sometimes they get mad at us. That's OK. Their well-being is more important than the feeling of the moment. We persist in enforcing physical, spiritual, and emotional safety because we care—we have in the past and will do the same in the future. We work to earn and protect the trust of our children. The older they become, the more we realize that, although we can suggest, guide, pray, and command, they will make their own choices. We hope they choose to trust us. More important, we hope our children learn to trust God.

The love we feel for our children is a mere hint of the concern God feels for us. He loves us because we are. He wants our trust and delights in our growth. He works for our physical, emotional, and spiritual joy. Even when we disobey Him or betray Him, He continually works to bring us back to Him and to the happiness only He can give.

God too gives us rules to help us find the contentment we seek. He offers laws that show us the way things are—laws that teach us about the nature of people, the nature of sin, the importance of right choices. These laws are designed to keep us from danger, bring us joy, and guide us to freedom; not to punish us, take away our fun, or hinder our choices. Nothing delights God more than when we respond to Him and trust Him.

Like a good parent, God has given and continues to give His life for us. He offers the power to choose the path that brings joy and freedom to us and those we encounter. With His advice and help, we can understand His rules.

Unlike a parent, though, God never lets us down, never stops loving, never loses His patience, and never makes a mistake. He always knows exactly what to do. God cherishes our trust, not because He has an ego to serve, but because obeying Him leads us to love and joy.

Christianity is a relationship similar to the parent-child bond. Almighty God wants to know and love us. In most religions, people try to find God and earn a place with Him. But in Christianity, God has found us and invites us to respond to Him. Once we accept God through the person Jesus Christ, we are free to please Him with our trust, not because we have to keep on His good side. We have our whole lives to get to know God and to learn to live for Him. This incredible journey begins the moment we trust Him in faith. It continues as we trust Him for advice, comfort, security, and companionship. Take the step of faith now or deepen the relationship you've already started.

Notice the beauty of relationship: love for a person is more powerful than love for a set of religious principles. Love for a person is a better motivator than the rightness of the person's rule. Love for a person invites response, service, and loyalty. God's love is immeasurable, indescribable, unimaginable. He has given His very life for us.

❧ LIVE GOD'S WORD ❧

1. Memorize Romans 3:21-24. Write in your journal how this makes you feel toward God. Toward yourself. Toward other church members. Toward persons of other denominations. Toward non-Christians.
2. Though human relationships can never approximate our relationship with God, they can teach us much about Him. Name a person whose love for you reminds you of God's love. Describe what this relationship teaches you about God. Thank this person for teaching you about God and His love.
3. Christians frequently speak of having and doing faith. What do they mean when they say someone has faith? Does faith? Begin a list of faith actions or faith illustrations. Write at least 5 but keep adding until you have more than 20. Notice the simplicity yet complexity of faith, its everydayness yet its specialness. Compare your list of actions to those in Romans 3–4.
4. Faith is not easy to put into words, for it is both an action and an attitude, both a response and an expression of need. After soaking yourself in Romans 3–4 and studying your list from the previous activity, sculpt, paint, or stitch a symbol of faith. Use the materials most familiar to you. If no concrete idea comes to you, shape a pipe cleaner or piece of aluminum foil until it looks like faith. Thank God for the insight He provides.
5. A religion is a striving for God according to a set of rules. A relationship is a series of responses and growing understandings. Relationships require contact, communication, and continuation. Write or talk to God about how the two of you have improved (or could improve) your contact, communication, and continuation.
6. Invite a friend who is cool toward Christianity to tell you what she doesn't like about it. Let her know on which points you agree with her. Let your agreement form a foundation for introducing Jesus as a relationship, not a religion. This may take two or more encounters.

CHAPTER FOUR

THROUGH SUFFERING
WITH
Grace

🍂 *LISTEN TO GOD'S WORD* 🍂

"I just don't understand why God let this happen," said Regina. "I had to miss the church mission trip because I was laid up in the hospital with a broken leg in traction. I know it was God's will that I go on that trip."

Regina had been painting a two-story house without safety equipment when she fell. Her fall was due to her own negligence, not God's plan. Why do we blame God for harm we bring on ourselves? Why do we give God "credit" for another's cruel choice? Why do we assume everything that happens is His will? Consider that God might be as disappointed as we are about tragedies that happen. Not allowing sadness or evil to have the last word, He works to correct it; Paul explains in Romans 5:1-21 that God has taken the tragedy of sin and redeemed it through His Son.

God takes the daily sufferings that come directly or indirectly from our sinful world and turns them into perseverance, character, and hope. He neither causes tragedies to occur nor takes pleasure in them. But He will have the last word over them. When evil opposes His plan, He works to redeem it. As you study this Romans passage, find freedom from blaming God and freedom to hope in Him.

Read Romans 5:1-21.

1. Peace in happy and sad times alike comes through being rightly related to God through justification (Rom. 5:1). When God declares a repentant sinner justified, she can say, "It's *just-as-if-I'd* not sinned." How does justification give you peace no matter what the circumstances?

2. Notice the words "access," "stand," and "hope" in verse 2. We have direct access to God because of Jesus Christ. We stand on a firm foundation in Christ. We have certain hope of future glory. Which fact is most important to you? Why?

3. The rejoicing that comes in the midst of such suffering is not a giddy happiness but an irrefutable confidence in God. Tell how your access, stand, and hope enable you to "rejoice in [your] suffering" (v. 3).

4. Using your own biblical insight, define these terms.
Perseverance (see vv. 3-4):

Character (see v. 4):

Hope (see vv. 4-5):

Supplement your insights with a Bible concordance or Bible dictionary.

5. Describe a time God worked through your suffering to produce perseverance, character, and hope.

Do you find it easier to tell your own story of perseverance, character, and hope or to listen to someone else's? Why?

Is it a good idea to point out to a suffering friend the perseverance, character, and hope which are developing within her? Why or why not?

6. Read Romans 5:6-11, substituting your name for the words "we," "the ungodly," "a righteous man," and "us." Why does Jesus' death demonstrate God's love for you? Why does it give you security in both happy and sad times?

How do the truths in verses 6-11 make you even more certain of your access to Him, your secure stand in Him, and your hope in Him? How does your lifestyle show your certainty?

7. "Reconcile" means to restore a relationship with someone (see v. 10). Being reconciled is closely tied to being justified (see vv. 1, 9). How did Jesus' death reconcile you to God? How does His life reconcile you?

8. Romans 5:9-10 refers specifically to the final judgment. Words like "saved from God's wrath through [Jesus]" could make God and Jesus sound like adversaries. Why is this reasoning wrong, according to verse 8?

9. God will not allow sin and the suffering it causes to triumph. Write one or more Bible phrases from verses 12-21 which show an action of God that overcame the following elements of the sin problem.

Sin entered the world through the trespass of one man:

Death came to all through sin:

Judgment followed sin and brought condemnation:

Death reigned:

Sin increased:

Sin reigned in death:

What bothers you most about sin? What pleases you most about the remedy for it?

10. Sin is more rebellion against God and exaltation of self than it is a list of specific wrongs. Like Adam, we have chosen to rebel against God (see Rom. 3:23). Notice that sin expresses itself in actions called trespasses (vv. 15-18, 20). Name trespasses you commit. How do these trespasses demonstrate rebellion against God or exaltation of yourself?

11. What are the differences between "the gift of God" and "the trespass," according to verses 15-19?

12. In verse 19, "sinners" and "righteous" are terms of relationship, not behavior. While sin throws everything out of order, righteousness

sets it straight. Just as certainly as we experience the consequences of sin, we can experience life in Christ. What words and actions in your life show you are "made righteous" rather than "made [a] sinner"?

13. Romans 5:1-21 overviews the complicated conflict between sin and righteousness, disobedience and obedience. No matter how severe the battle gets, there is always a surplus of God's grace. Tell about a time when you experienced this personally.

Obviously, the best choice is to avoid sin altogether. However, when you do make a wrong choice, God will work to redeem it through His grace. Name a time when He did so for you.

14. Sometimes this conflict between sin and righteousness is an indirect one, a result of living in our sinful world. Many illnesses and catastrophes, for example, have no direct link with specific sins. How have you experienced peace, access, a place to stand, hope, and joy in the midst of an experience like this?

How do you know that righteousness will win? (See vv. 3-21.)

For Further Study
Read Genesis 1–3 to discover how "sin entered the world through one man" (Rom. 5:12). Read the Gospel of Mark to discover how "God's grace and the gift that came by the grace of the one man, Jesus Christ, overflow[ed] to the many" (Rom. 5:15).

LIFE EXAMPLE:
❧ God Is the Source of Rejoicing ❧

"God gave Sarah to you because you're such good parents," said a well-meaning friend after we discovered my eleven-month-old's hearing loss. I held my tongue but wanted to say, "The God I know is a loving Father who is the giver of all good gifts [James 1:17]. What kind of reward is hearing loss? Why would God give Sarah a disability that would make it hard for her to communicate with people and hard to learn about His world?"

Six years later, I still don't see the hearing loss as a gift. I'm not mad. I'm not bitter. I'm simply convinced that God dislikes hearing loss as much as we do. Just as I'm certain God did not give Sarah hearing loss, I'm certain that He is working with her to redeem it. He equips Sarah to find full happiness in the midst of limited hearing. He continuously lets her know of her worth and helps her focus on her abilities. He gives her eagerness and confidence which put other people at ease. He provides competent people to teach her listening and talking skills. He grants the knowledge that enables technologists to develop sophisticated hearing aids so Sarah can hear the most sounds possible. These are God's gifts, not the hearing loss. Thanks to them, most people don't even realize Sarah wears hearing aids or struggles to talk clearly. She's at the top of her class at school, thrives on learning, and makes friends with ease. She trusts Jesus and wants to make Him happy.

God's gifts are not sufferings; instead, they are the ability to overcome barriers, the joy that comes in the midst of frustration, the sensitivity that brings closeness, the delight that comes from knowing and trusting Him no matter what the circumstances. God and His gifts make us "rejoice in our sufferings."

Sarah's hearing loss is not good; but God, who enables her to love, listen, and learn in spite of hearing loss, is good. Sarah may always have difficulty hearing in a noisy room or understanding over the drone of an airplane. Still, we are absolutely confident that God's power will always be stronger than her frustrations. She may never be able to use an unamplified telephone, but we are positive that she'll hear every detail once she gets to heaven. Suffering is bad, but it's temporary. God is good, and He's permanent. God Himself, not the suffering, is the cause for rejoicing (Rom. 5:3).

God is in the redeeming business. He refuses to let evil or sadness have the last word. He persistently works with us to bring good into the middle of tragedy, to overcome evil with good. We live in a world where people have chosen to sin, and their sins have messed up the goodness God intended for this world. Sin in its essence is rebellion against God. As such, sin creates havoc and heartache for all who choose to commit it and for the innocent ones around them.

Romans 5:1-21 is a lovely picture of God's overcoming evil to bring good. He invites each of us to make a fresh start through justification and a close relationship with Him (see vv. 1-2). He works in the midst of suffering to bring permanent perseverance, tried and true character, and certain hope (see vv. 3-5). He came in Jesus to reconcile us to Himself (see vv. 6-11). He brought life, grace, and righteousness into a world of sin (see vv. 12-21).

When circumstances get bad, we can choose sin, despair, and self-sufficiency; or we can choose life, grace, and righteousness. Sarah's hearing loss is not a result of her sin or anyone else's. But it comes from living in a sinful world, marred by imperfections. While sin is strong, God is stronger. His grace will always enable Sarah to obtain and understand the information she needs (see vv. 20-21).

🕮 *LIVE GOD'S WORD* 🕮

1. Memorize Romans 5:1-2. Notice that peace (see v. 1) is as much an action as a feeling. List words and actions you use to express your peace with God.
2. Read Romans 5:6-11. Write a letter in your journal to Jesus, thanking Him for living and dying for you. If you run out of things to say, read verses 6-11 one more time.
3. Walk through your house, your neighborhood, your office, or another familiar place to find objects that illustrate sin and grace. How do objects and examples help you understand these complex but crucial realities?
4. How do you feel about Adam? Jot down words, colors, emotions that come to you as you think about him. Recall that he is not the only one responsible for sin. Every person since Adam, except Jesus Christ, has chosen to sin. Now write your thoughts again.
5. Paraphrase Romans 5:12-21, translating religious-sounding words such as "sin," "trespass," "grace," and "righteousness" into everyday language. Use a Bible dictionary to deepen your insight.
6. Avoid making heroes of those who suffer, or assuming suffering is a reward for strong faith (see vv. 3-5). Suffering doesn't come to those who are already strong. God provides power for each suffering as it comes. First Corinthians 10:13 is often misquoted as, "God will give you only what you can handle." Instead, God makes each person strong enough to face the difficulties that come to him or her. Reread 1 Corinthians 10:13, particularly, "He will also provide a way out."

    Rather than interpreting the suffering for a friend in pain with verses like Romans 5:3-5, invite her to tell her story. Ask questions like, "How is God helping you through this?" rather than "What blessings are you experiencing as a result of what you are going through?"

CHAPTER FIVE

FROM BAD HABITS TO *Loving Actions*

❧ LISTEN TO GOD'S WORD ❧

We usually think of death as a sad and agonizing experience. Death may be agonizing, but it doesn't have to be sad, especially when it is the type of death described in Romans 6:1-14. There Paul urges us to die to sin. This sounds wonderfully holy, but can be horribly difficult when sin has become a persistent habit. The persistence of a particular sin can make it hard to imagine life without it. The persistence (and familiarity) of a sin makes it seem less evil than it is. The persistence of a sin makes us hesitate to even try to get rid of it. But there's good news! Find freedom from destructive habits in Romans 6:1-14.

Read Romans 6:1-14.
1. Paul's teaching that God loves us no matter what we do and that salvation is a free gift led some people to assume they could sin freely and thus earn more grace (see Rom. 5:20). Why is this belief incorrect? Why bother being good if God will forgive us for sins? (See 6:1-4, 21.)

   Following God makes life safe in the same way obeying traffic laws makes travel safe. Give examples of God's laws which bring physical safety, emotional safety, and spiritual safety. Name sins in each category which do the opposite.

2. Grace is not a reason to take advantage of God, but a reason to hope. Tell how and why this is so (see vv. 1-4).

3. Why are Christians baptized? To what does baptism testify? (See vv. 3-4.)

Physical baptism is a beautiful picture of dying to sin (going under the water) and rising to new life (coming out of the water). How do you demonstrate these same principles as you live your "new life" with Jesus Christ?

4. The best part about dying to sin is being able to live to something better. In the future, this will be resurrection (see v. 5). In the present, it is a new life (see vv. 4, 6-7). What expressions of this new life came to you when you died to a specific sin habit? What new habit took its place?

The "body of sin" in verse 6 is not our physical body but every action, attitude, and thought that is opposed to God. Name a physical action and a nonphysical action you do that are sin. Choose to let Jesus do away with these.

5. Notice the "if" in verse 5. Verses 5-7 address death while verses 8-10 address life. Why must death with Christ come before life with Him?

6. Even death has no power over Jesus (vv. 8-10). How do you demonstrate that death no longer has mastery over you?

7. Living a new life in Christ is a direct expression of our relationship with Him. When we fail to live by God's ethics and morals, it is not because we did not have His power, but because we did not call on it (see vv. 11-14). Explain why this is true.

8. Dying to sin is a series of choices. Sin is always available. We can't always stop sin's initial entry, but we can keep it from remaining. Name a way you push sin out of your life (see v. 12).

9. A second way to die to sin is to not let it happen — to purposely stop the body part involved in the sin (such as closing a gossipy mouth). Name a way you have been an instrument of wickedness. Name a way you became an instrument of righteousness instead (see v. 13).

10. A third way to die to sin is to deny its mastery. Sin is powerful but it doesn't have to control you because God's grace is stronger. Name a way you give God, rather than sin, mastery in your life (see v. 14).

11. The sin battle is a tough one because we are now living between our redemption and our resurrection. Which action or principle in 6:1-14 makes it easiest for you to offer yourself to God in this imperfect world?

12. We often call a pattern of sin a "bad habit." Because our old self has died with Christ, we don't have to be slaves to bad habits (see vv. 6-7). Name a bad habit Jesus has freed you from or could free you from. How might another Christian help you get rid of your bad habit? How would living the principles in the verses below help you?

Verses 1-4:

Verses 5-7:

Verses 8-10:

Verses 11-12:

Verses 13-14:

For Further Study
Continue your study of question 1 by examining Romans 3 and 6:15-23. Continue your study of question 12 by examining Ephesians 4:17-32 and Colossians 3:1-17.

LIFE EXAMPLE:
❧ Words that Wound ❧

"I can't believe they picked you. They must not know you very well!"
"How could you be so stupid as to forget that?"
"What a ridiculous idea! What ever made you think that would work?"
"What! You spilled it! I can't depend on you for anything!"
"It's about time you got a raise!"

These are the things Cathy (name changed) says to the people she loves the most—her husband, her children, her friends at church. She doesn't want to hurt people's feelings, but the words just come out. She can't seem to stop them. Cathy confesses, "As a parent, I should be the strongest encourager of my children. Instead I put them down at every opportunity. As a church friend, I should give words of love; instead, I come across as jealous and touchy. As a wife, I should dwell on the strengths of my husband, not the weaknesses. But I turn even the good he does into an opportunity to criticize."

Cathy has developed a sin habit. Her criticism habit discourages, destroys, and divides. She learned to criticize when her parents criticized her. Though she vowed never to make people feel the way her parents made her feel, she finds herself repeating their patterns. Television shows that encourage ridicule as a way to solve problems reinforce Cathy's criticism habit. She hears criticism and cuts so often that they sound OK. But they're not. Criticism makes people doubt the good which God created in them, decreases their confidence and capability, destroys their motivation to try, and makes them feel hated by the very people who should care.

The truths found in Romans 6:1-14 can help Cathy and you in the struggle to turn bad habits into loving ones. Ponder one of your own sinful habits as you learn how these principles turn the habit of criticism into the habit of encouragement.

☐ *Die to the sin* (see vv. 1-4)   Once Cathy discovers the destructiveness of her criticism habit, she can refuse to continue it. Even though everyone around her criticizes and even though she doesn't mean to harm anyone, criticism still hurts. Seeing criticism as the sin it is motivates Cathy to get rid of it.

☐ *Make new choices* (see v. 4) Even after Cathy decides to stop criticizing, she won't find it easy. Curtailing criticism becomes easier by putting another action in its place. Cathy can replace criticism with genuine compliments and encouraging words.

☐ *Work together with Jesus to correct the habit* (see vv. 5-7) As Jesus helps Cathy discover the reason for her criticism, where she learned it, and how to stop it, He frees her from that sin. Because Cathy's old self was crucified with Christ, she is no longer a slave to criticism or any other sin. With Christ's power, she can control the habit, rather than letting it control her. Cathy can love and encourage with her words instead of discouraging and creating pain.

☐ *Refuse to let the habit master you* (see vv. 8-10, 14) Habits are hard to break. When Cathy is tempted to criticize, she remembers that Christ, not criticism, is her master. Living to Christ means the habit no longer has ultimate power and that she can love others like Jesus does.

☐ *Be deliberate* (see vv. 11-14) Every time Cathy sees her children, husband, or friends, she consciously offers words of encouragement. She stops critical words before they can leave her mouth by thinking them through first. She deliberately refuses to offer her mouth to sin as an instrument of wickedness, but offers it to righteousness instead. Cathy keeps her mouth closed until she can think of a genuine compliment or vote of confidence. When she speaks compliments, cuts have a hard time slipping in.

Cathy won't solve her criticism habit in one or two tries because the power of sin is strong (see study 6). But deliberately dying to the old habit in order to live to the new one can release the love she and her family crave.

Put the principles from Romans 6:1-14 into practice in your own life. Begin by listing your sin habits. Then use steps like those described above to (1) list ways of dying to sin, (2) write how to live to new life, and (3) take specific actions to bring about change.

For example, if you overeat:

1. die to the need to munch all the time by finding something else to do (such as chewing gum or doing handwork);
2. live to feeling good about your body;
3. keep the chocolate out of the house so you won't be tempted.

Or, if you're continually late:

1. die to the worry about getting there early and having nothing to do;
2. live to people being able to count on you;
3. leave earlier than usual to compensate for lateness.

Let God's love be your motivation as you discover and live your new life.

❧ LIVE GOD'S WORD ❧

1. Memorize Romans 6:4. During this week, keep a list of every evidence you see of the new life God is growing in you. Examples might include the ability to show love in a way you hadn't been able to before, the peace you feel even in the midst of a problem, the pleasure you notice in genuine friendship, the confidence you feel about God's love for you, the sweetness you enjoy in a conversation with a child, or the intricacy you see in God's creation.

2. As you invite God to help you die to sin and live to new life, be patient. Researchers have discovered that it takes about 6 weeks to change a bad habit. Some call this the "40-Day Test." If you can avoid a bad habit for about 40 days, it ceases to be a habit. Similarly, if you can do a good action regularly for 40 days, it becomes a good habit. Rather than trying to change an action "forever," aim first to pass the "40-Day Test."

3. Noticing others' sin habits can make you feel safe, even superior. Each time you notice another's sin habit, deliberately pinpoint one of your own. This practice not only keeps you humble, but it focuses your attention on your own actions.

4. Notice ways that God is bringing new life to fellow Christians (see Rom. 6:4, 8). Send notes to these believers and point out the good you see God doing in them. Mention the way they love, how they demonstrate a fruit of the Spirit, or otherwise show that they live with Christ. This encouragement can celebrate the fact that Christianity is a daily journey of joy.

   Note: Compliments are most effective when given in good times. Complimenting virtues during sad times can make it seem that you take the trouble lightly.

CHAPTER SIX

FROM BATTLING SIN TO *Overcoming It*

❦ *LISTEN TO GOD'S WORD* ❦

"I can't figure out what is wrong. I was sincere when I gave my heart to Jesus, but I still do wrong. I thought I had a fresh start, but the same bad habits continue to trouble me. I thought sin would no longer appeal to me once I had accepted Jesus, but I can't do the good I want to do. What's wrong with me?"

The teaching that sin will lose its appeal when you become a Christian doesn't pan out in real life. Experience indicates that Satan works all the harder to make sin attractive. Even when we commit to obey God in a certain area, we still have trouble carrying through. First pinpoint the sins that badger you to the point of discouragement. Then find freedom from this discouragement as you seek the solution in Romans 7:14–8:4.

Read Romans 7:14–8:4.

1. Spiritually speaking, what do you do that you don't want to do? What do you *not* do that you actually want to do?

2. This agonizing battle between spiritual and unspiritual action is based in sin (see 7:16-20). Sin is the ignoring of or rebellion against God. Paul saw the Law as good and spiritual (originating from God) because it makes specific sins apparent and points us to our need for a solution to sin (see Rom. 5:20; 7:12). What do you like about God's Law? (See Ex. 20:1-17.)

Why is it not strong enough to help you be good?

49

Why is agreeing with God's Law the first step to obeying it?

3. Keeping in mind the sins you listed in question 1, how does doing wrong enslave you rather than free you? (See 7:14.)

Read Romans 7:25. How does submitting to God free you rather than enslave you?

4. Why do you suppose sin keeps trying to live in us after we understand its dangers? Even after we become Christians? (See vv. 17-19.)

On this side of heaven, our old sinful nature and our new life in Christ exist side by side, the sinful nature frantically trying to keep its place. How might the devil use this uncomfortable reality to discourage you? To keep you from fighting sin? To doubt God's love for you?

Ultimately, our new life in Christ will triumph. We live the triumph day by day as we choose to obey God rather than sin. How can God use this to encourage you? Empower you? Help you continue to triumph?

5. Paul depicted the battle with sin as a war between his mind (inner self) and his actions (outer self) (see 7:21-23). Others call it a struggle between our carnal side (opposed to God) and our spiritual side (in harmony with God). Still others picture an angel sitting on one shoulder and a devil on the other, both whispering into a person's ear. Draw or describe a picture which makes the conflict between sin and obedience clear to you.

6. Paul felt wretched in 7:24. List at least three words that describe your feelings when you wage battle against wrongdoing and lose.

Do you have to get to this desperate point before you are ready to accept God's power? Why or why not?

7. Verse 25 begins a discussion of the solution. Notice the Law of God and the law of sin in this verse. Read Galatians 5:16-17. How does Jesus Christ influence the law you choose to give yourself to?

8. Read about the law of the Spirit of life in Romans 8:1-4; then review the law of sin in 7:14-25. List the characteristics and results of each law.

When do you submit to the law of sin? Why?

When do you submit to the law of the Spirit? Why?

9. Jesus Himself is the key to freedom from sin. Because this truth is so powerful, sing, draw, or recite in the form of poetry the words of Romans 8:1-2.

How will your freedom from condemnation and your freedom to live by the Spirit impact your life today? This week?

10. Why is sin stronger than you? Why is God stronger than sin? Name specific actions you will take to tap into God's power (see 8:3).

11. Note that the "righteous requirements" (8:4) means that righteousness is required, not that the requirements are righteous. No human explanation fully captures the meaning of the Incarnation (God in flesh) and atonement (creation of conditions that make it possible to be "at one" with God). But words can help us understand. Based on 8:3-4, explain the Incarnation and the Atonement in words, pictures, or symbols.

12. Reread your answers to question 1. How can the Holy Spirit correct this problem for you? Write the specific actions, words, and attitudes to which He is directing you.

For Further Study

1. Paul addressed difficult questions in Romans 7–8, such as: "Why can't we control our actions?" and "Why do Christians struggle with doing right?" Sin is at the center of these problems. Do you see sin as a power, a personality, a characteristic? How do we fight it? Learn what the Bible has to say about the nature of sin by studying verses you find in a concordance under *sin*.

2. Some Bible students say Paul described in 7:14-24 his life before accepting Christ. The present-tense verbs ("I am," "I do") and absence of spiritual conflict in other descriptions of Paul's life before conversion make others think these verses describe Paul's life after accepting Christ. Which seems more likely to you, and why? Read the entire Book of Romans (especially 5:1–8:39); then make your decision.

LIFE EXAMPLE:
✿ Choose to Show God's Love ✿

"I love my son, I really do," said Rebecca (name changed), "but I just can't seem to be the mother he needs. He's unruly and disrespectful to most adults. I know his anger at me is a cry for help. I know his disobedience is a request for some kind of control in his life. I know consistent discipline is the answer. I know real love would give the help, control, and discipline he craves. But I just can't bring myself to give them.

"Lately he's had trouble getting his homework done. He stays up late, becomes frustrated, and then does poor work or none at all. He had a science project due Monday. I told him the Monday before that he would have to finish by Thursday if he wanted to spend Friday night at Jacob's. I knew he'd be worn out Saturday because they stay up late, and that Sunday would be too busy to allow for homework. He agreed.

"Friday afternoon came and the project was not finished. I reminded him of our agreement and told him he'd have to stay home and finish. He became angry and said, 'I never get time to be with my friends. Nobody in his right mind would do homework on a Friday night! This isn't fair, Mom, and you know it.' For two hours he walked from room to room slamming doors and sulking. The tension in the house was horrible.

"I went from having the confidence that his choice had created this circumstance to feeling like the meanest mother in the world. Maybe he did need a break, I thought. Finally, I could stand it no longer. He wasn't getting anything done on the science project anyway, so I let him go to Jacob's. He won. I know he sulked around in order to get me to give in. I know I should have held my ground, but I didn't. Why can't I do it?" wondered Rebecca.

Real life is hard. And the sins that make it hard aren't always the major ones—murder, theft, adultery. Instead, they have names like Inconsistency, Anger, Insecurity, Manipulation, Doubt, and Fear. These pervasive and powerful sins seem to sap our energy and make it impossible to obey God. Rebecca, the mother in the story above, struggled to give her son consistent discipline. Her son's anger and manipulation made her doubt her wisdom. His demands made her worry about hurting him. He wanted limits, but she felt powerless to give them. Letting him bend the rules made him more anxious, not more cooperative. Both mother and son struggled without success to love each other.

Everyday struggles like these are easy to put into words but hard to solve. We feel the need for a superhuman power. Thanks to God we have that power—His name is the Holy Spirit. He offers us power to do what we are too weak to do (see Rom. 8:1-3).

Rebecca is a dedicated Christian and knows the Holy Spirit is available. Why does she find it so hard to use His power? *Because sin is strong.*

Recognizing the strength of sin is the first step in winning the battle. The subsequent steps vary from situation to situation. Rebecca might need the Holy Spirit's power expressed through a friend or her spouse to whom she could make herself accountable. When tempted to give in to her son's demands, she might telephone her friend or spouse for support. Or she could tap into the Holy Spirit's power by stopping long enough to think through how she would explain her actions to her friend or spouse.

Rebecca might also ask the Spirit to help her see the good that results when she gives consistent guidelines. Specifically, her son reacts strongly but then calms down and does his work; he fusses when she gives directives but seems to find security in the limits; he resists for hours with the first discipline, for minutes with the second, and not at all after several consistent applications. As Rebecca gives the Holy Spirit opportunity to work, she sees His power.

The battle to love and live as God wants us to is not easy, but it can be won. Sin is strong, *but the Spirit is stronger.*

❧ LIVE GOD'S WORD ❧

1. Memorize Romans 8:1. Each time you recite it, put your name in the place of "those." Write in your journal how you will live out this status.
2. What sins do you struggle with? What steps does the Holy Spirit recommend for utilizing His power? Write a letter from the Holy Spirit addressed to you, reminding yourself of truths in Romans 7:14–8:4 and of ways to implement them.
3. The next time you become frustrated with a friend, coworker, family member, or church member, recall the nature of the struggle with sin. How might this person be trying to do well but failing? Pray Romans 8:1-2 for this person.
4. Get together with a trusted and sensitive friend. Share an area in which you struggle to be the person God wants you to be. Invite her in a sensitive way to do the same. Share ideas on how the Holy Spirit might help you and your friend. Reread *Life Example* in study 6 for a sample.

CHAPTER SEVEN

THROUGH SADNESS WITH *Security*

❧ *LISTEN TO GOD'S WORD* ❧

Does sadness over our suffering contradict our faith? Not at all. Sadness can be a sign of faith, not a denial of it. Sadness is an expression that things are not as they should be, that we trust God to make them better, and that we want to work with Him to make it so. Sadness is an acknowledgment that this world is not our home and that there's a better day coming. In Romans 8:17, Paul explained that Christians participate in both the suffering and the glory of Jesus Christ. Now in Romans 8:18-39, he explains four truths that can carry us through suffering: (1) Christians have certain hope for a glorious future; (2) pain is a precursor to a beautiful result; (3) the Holy Spirit feels with us and prays for us; (4) nothing can separate us from the love and care of God.

Underline these and other powerful promises as you read this Scripture. Then invite Jesus to help you live by them when you suffer or walk with a hurting friend through suffering. Find freedom from needing an explanation for everything, and freedom to be secure in the midst of suffering.

Read Romans 8:18-39.

1. C.K. Barrett phrases the first part of verse 18, "The glory is as sure as the suffering" (*The Epistle to the Romans*, p. 165). The fact of future glory puts present suffering in perspective. Even so, the pain is now. How do you think God wants you to respond to suffering while you're going through it?

2. We live in an imperfect world. Just as certain as present imperfection are future perfection and redemption. Verses 19-21 voice the expectation that gets us through present suffering. Describe this expectation of glory in your own words.

3. Like a woman in labor, nature and people groan and wait and hope (see vv. 22-23). How is our wait for the final day like the wait for a child's birth?

What groanings do you see in creation? In your life?

How does the result (final redemption) make the pain bearable?

4. During present sufferings, we have the Holy Spirit to help us through. Verse 23 declares we have the "firstfruits" of the Spirit, a type of down payment and pledge that we will realize the glory of final salvation. How do we know this hope is real and not just wishful thinking?

Besides giving hope, how else does the Holy Spirit help you through suffering?

5. Sometimes it's hard to know what or how to pray when we are in pain. Read verses 26-27 for the solution to this problem. Describe it.

Let the Holy Spirit pray for you now. Jot down feelings, words, or images that come to you.

6. What insight into 8:28 do you gain from verses 29-38?

"God works for good" means that He can bring good into bad situations, not that He turns bad into good or that everything that happens is good. Name a time God worked good into one of your bad experiences.

7. Verses 29-30 describe the good toward which God is working. The verses trace God's actions to draw people to Himself. How have you experienced God calling you to Himself?

How have you experienced Him conforming you to the likeness of His Son?

How does this process continue even when bad or sad things happen?

8. Answer these questions from verses 31-32:

"If God is for us, who can be against us?"

"He who did not spare His own Son, but gave Him up for us all—how will He not also, along with Him, graciously give us all things?"

9. Imagine being in a courtroom where someone is challenging your security in Jesus Christ (see vv. 33-34). Who is this person or what is the circumstance that accuses you? How do you defend yourself?

How does God defend you?

10. Psalm 44:22 foretold the sufferings of Christians and is quoted in Romans 8:36. First-century Christians faced persecution under Nero. Today believers face other dangers. Read verses 35-37. Without worrying about fine distinctions between types of problems, name an event, experience, or fear in each category below that has threatened to separate you from the love of Christ. Then name a way Christ enables you to be "more than [a] conqueror" in the midst of it.

	EVENT	WAY TO CONQUER
Trouble		
Hardship		
Persecution		
Famine		
Nakedness		
Danger		
Sword		

Why do you know verse 37 is true?

11. The threats in verse 35 were not as frightening to some first-century Christians as the unseen powers listed in verse 38. Which in each pair do you consider the greater threat to your security or happiness? Why?

Death or life:

Angels or demons:

Present or the future:

Height or depth:

A power or something else in creation:

Why is God's love stronger than each of these? (See vv. 38-39.)

12. Review these promises from Romans 8:18-39 that minister to us during pain. Write why you need each.

    ☐ A future glory will replace present suffering (see vv. 18-21).

    ☐ Groaning will be replaced with the fulfillment of our hope (see vv. 22-25).

    ☐ The Holy Spirit understands us and prays for us when we can't put our needs, thoughts, or feelings into words (see vv. 26-27).

    ☐ Nothing—no person, place, pain, experience, or object—can separate us from the love of God (see vv. 35-39).

For Further Study
Use a Bible concordance to read verses that contain "foreknew," "predestined," "called," "justified," and "glorified" (Rom. 8:29-30). Let the Bible teach you what these words mean. Study one word at a time.

LIFE EXAMPLE:
❦ Pain Is Not the Opposite of Faith ❦

Three-year-old Amy (name changed) brought delight every time she walked into the room. She used words beyond her years to tell about the adventures in her life or to sing songs about Jesus. Her smiles and precociousness belied the fact that she battled leukemia. Just about the time she whipped the leukemia, an aggressive bacteria stole her life.

The people who knew Amy anguished over her death. They cried to express their loneliness for her. They raged at the illness that took such a bright, affectionate, and joy-producing child. They grieved for all that Amy would never experience. They yearned for one more hug.

Perhaps most deeply affected was Amy's mother, Nancy. Nancy knew more certainly than anyone that God had not let death steal her child. She recalls clearly the moment that Amy was no longer in her body, the moment Amy went to heaven. He scooped up Amy and brought her into His glorious presence.

Even though Nancy knows all these things, she still hurts. But why? Where is her faith? Nancy's faith is as strong and solid as ever. Her faith is exactly the vehicle that takes her through this crisis. She knows that just as God is cradling Amy in His arms, He is there for Nancy and her family, sustaining them as they live each minute on earth without Amy. Nancy depends on God to strengthen her, to walk beside her, to guide her through her days without Amy, to lead her through the tough choices ahead. Nancy leans on God and finds comfort as He cries along with her. She knows He is working in her life to redeem the tragedy that has occurred (see Rom. 8:28).

But if Nancy knows all these things, why does she struggle? Why doesn't her trust in God keep away the anguish? Simply because pain and faith are not opposites. Pain is an expression of our Christianity. The believer's pain shows how in touch she is with people, with life, with love. Persons worth loving are worth agonizing over.

Remember Jesus' sadness when Lazarus died? Jesus knew He would raise Lazarus within a few minutes after He reached the tomb, but He still hurt (John 11:35). As 1 Peter 4:12-19 explains, suffering should not seem strange to Christians; it's a part of our life on earth. Being Christian doesn't mean we bury our feelings, pretend that everything is OK, and call that faith. It means we stay in touch with what matters, depend on God's power, and fully experience every event of life.

It's possible that Nancy and other Christians suffer pain more intensely than nonbelievers simply because many believers feel everything more deeply. Jesus brings life into focus and adds clarity to every experience.

Nancy knows that the way to get through pain is to feel it, to stand firmly on God as her foundation, and to rest, knowing that He understands and feels along with her. She doesn't need easy answers or smoothly worked-out explanations because she depends on the source of those answers, God Himself. He gives her the solid hope that gets her through her pain and her family's pain. She agonizes over separation from the one she shared nearly every waking moment with. Nancy hurts too for Carol, Amy's sister—knowing that no one can replace Amy in Carol's life as a sister, playmate, confidante. Nancy hurts too for her husband Jason; she remembers the delight Amy brought when she used to crawl up on his lap while he drank his morning coffee. This pain is excruciating. But one day it will end (see Rev. 21:4).

Faith means we have a hope that gets us through pain. It's trusting God feels pain along with us. It's the ability to go on living and loving, giving and receiving. Nancy continues to care, meet Carol's needs, and reach others for Jesus. Evil cannot steal her joy. Settled comfortably beneath her grief is a solid foundation of faith that won't be shaken.

God refuses to let tragedies overwhelm us. Romans 8:28 promises that God will work good into any tragedy. Amy's family and friends know that Amy's tragic death was a product of living in this imperfect world. Just as certainly, they know that God's love can overpower the sadness and bring joy in the midst of it. Those who knew Amy had the joy of delighting in her for three powerful years. They have the certainty of a future reunion with her in heaven. They have the security of knowing that God won't let trouble, hardship, persecution, famine, or anything else separate them from His love. Along with Amy's family, we can be certain that "neither death nor life, neither angels nor demons, neither the present nor the future, nor any powers, neither height nor depth, nor anything else in all creation, will be able to separate us from the love of God that is in Christ Jesus our Lord" (8:38-39).

❧ LIVE GOD'S WORD ❧

1. Memorize the verse from Romans 8:18-39 that speaks most strongly to you. Write in your journal how this verse has made or will make a difference in your understanding of God and in your life.
2. Write a letter to someone going through a time of sadness or pain. Let the letter express your love rather than offer a pat answer.
3. What amazes you most about Jesus: His death, His resurrection, or His intercession for you? (See v. 34.) Write a prayer of thanks to Him for these three love expressions and tell Him how each impacts you.
4. Quoting Scripture promises to someone who is hurting can come across as a faith put-down, as if to say, "If you were more spiritual, you wouldn't be hurting." Or the person may find it more irritating than encouraging. Instead of sharing your favorite promises, ask the hurting person to share a promise that she finds helpful.

CHAPTER EIGHT

FROM USELESSNESS TO

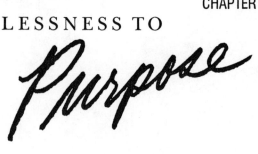

Purpose

❧ LISTEN TO GOD'S WORD ❧

A fulfilled woman has an intriguing job and a chore-doing family. She is busy but happy. She chooses one responsibility at church and does it well.	A fulfilled woman gives herself fully to her family and church. She is happy encouraging others and in doing her best. She doesn't need a paying job to be fulfilled.

Which is true? Both. How can both be true? Because different women have different gifts and because God guides each woman individually to fulfill His plans for her. The question women should ask themselves is: "Am I obeying God?" not "Am I fulfilling society's expectations for me?" As you study Romans 12:1-8, notice the variety of gifts God gives and ponder ways to express the ones you've received. Find freedom to fulfill God's expectations, and freedom from human expectations.

Read Romans 11:33–12:8.

  1. Jot down at least five actions or characteristics you adore about God. Then let Romans 11:33-36 help you add to your list.

  2. One way to show your adoration for God is to offer yourself to Him. Why is this the best way to please and worship God? (see 12:1)

How does "in view of God's mercy" (12:1) add to your motivation to offer yourself to God? Notice that this refers to God's mercy as described in the first 11 chapters of Romans.

3. Find four characteristics of your sacrifice to God in 12:1.

"Holy" (referring to Christians) means "set apart for dedication to God." It does not mean perfect. Name several ways you are holy.

4. A great threat to offering yourself to God is the pressure to be like other people. What pattern of the world currently molds you?

The solution to this threat is to let God mold you. What pattern of God has emerged (or could emerge) in you? (See 12:2; also 1 Peter 1:14-16.)

5. Why is a renewed-by-God mind important for discovering and understanding His will? (See 12:2.)

Find three characteristics of the will of God in 12:2. Why is each important to you?

6. Does your self-esteem tend to be too high or too low? (See v. 3.)

Why is thinking too highly of yourself opposite to the truths expressed in 12:4-5? Why is thinking too little of yourself opposite to these verses?

Why is thinking too much or too little of yourself a hindrance to spiritual service?

7. The "measure of faith" in 12:3 does not mean some have more faith than others, but that each Christian has a portion of faith sufficient for understanding and living God's will. Why is this faith the opposite of pride? How does it impact your view of yourself? Your purpose in the world?

8. This passage conveys two important truths concerning spiritual gifts: (1) God has given each Christian a specific gift (ability or power) that equips him or her for service; and (2) each gift is to be used for the good of the church. Why is each truth important to the other? (see vv. 3-6a)

God's grace empowers you to discover and live your gift. How do you feel about being gifted and guided to function as a meaningful part of the church?

9. In verses 6-8, Paul listed seven gifts. Write these seven and circle the one that is most important.

Deciding which gift is most important is as impossible as deciding what part of your physical body is most important. Think this through by selecting an important part of your physical body and an important person in your local church.

Now explain why the following parts of the body are important. Tell why your most important body part would have trouble doing without these parts.

Heart:

Skin:

Muscles:

Brain:

Bones:

Intestines, liver, and kidneys:

Did you name your pastor or another prominent leader as the most important person in your church? Tell why these roles in the church are equally crucial.

Bible teachers for preschool, children, youth, adults:

Servers:

Encouragers:

Nursery workers:

Janitors:

Givers:

How does seeing the physical body and the spiritual body (the church) as a whole minimize the temptation to rank one person above the other? (See 12:4-5.)

10. How smoothly does the body of Christ operate in your local church? Consider your church's spiritual gifts and pray for their effective use. Deepen understanding of each as you write answers across from the questions.

Prophets apply God's message to the lives of the people in the church and community. How do prophets in your church do this? (See v. 6.)

"Service" translates a word else-where rendered "ministry." Serv-ers help with unselfish motives. How do servers in your church do this? (See v. 7.)

Those with the gift of teaching make truth clear and challenging. Name a teacher who has done this for you. Describe this teach-er's teaching (see v. 7).

Encouragers motivate people to live God's way—to stop wrongs and start rights. What words have people used to encourage you to obey God? (See v. 8.) Has someone tried to encourage you but made you feel worse? Why did this happen? Was it bibli-cal encouragement?

Givers seldom feel used. They are more concerned with meeting needs. Why do they need God's grace to be givers? (See v. 8.)

A leader motivates individuals or groups to grow in Christ and to express that growth through love and service. Name a leader in your church, high or low pro-file, and describe how this person leads you (see v. 8).

Those with the gift of mercy re-spond sensitively and positively to those who are sick or needy (see v. 8). What expressions of mercy do you need when you are sick? Why is cheerfulness more effective than pity or duty?

11. Review the chart above and the *Life Example* section of study 8. Which gift do you think God has given you? Why do you think this is your gift?

How would your gift enable you to offer yourself as a living sacrifice to God? (See 12:1, 6-8.)

How could you use your gift in your church?

12. Your spiritual gift is a strong indicator of your daily purpose as well as your work at church. Name a way you could use your spiritual gift in a job (paid or volunteer), career, or other daily responsibility.

Write a dialogue between you and God where He discusses how He wants to fulfill you and fulfill others through you.

For Further Study
1. Learn from the experiences of women who have struggled to discover and use their God-given gifts. Choose biographies or magazines, such as *Today's Christian Woman*, that include features on well-known women and everyday heroes.
2. Consult books on spiritual gifts, such as *Unwrap Your Spiritual Gifts* by Kenneth O. Gangel (Wheaton, Ill.: Victor Books, 1983).

LIFE EXAMPLE:
❧ My Church Is Gifted ❧

What is your spiritual gift? How does God want you to serve Him through your church or outside your church? As you search for answers, recall these two important truths about spiritual gifts: (1) every Christian has at least one spiritual gift; and (2) gifts are to be used for the good of the church.

Determine how these truths work in your church by studying Romans 12:6-8 carefully and then examining the descriptions below. Ask yourself: *Which gift is mine? How do I use this gift for the good of the church?*

The Gifts
Prophesying. A prophet is more a forth-teller than a fortune teller or future teller. Prophets have the courage to speak for God even when doing so is unpopular. They can see how the Bible applies to life and can put this application into words people understand. Read Old Testament books like Isaiah and Micah to discover what prophets do. Pastors and Sunday School teachers often have the gift of prophecy.

Serving. A servant cares and loves. She doesn't mind doing whatever needs doing because she does it for God and His people. A servant emphasizes the practical and the specific. She doesn't object to working in the background to accomplish good things. A servant might be the one who serves the fellowship meals, cares for babies so their parents can concentrate during worship, or coordinates the youth snack suppers.

Teaching. Teachers explain what the Bible means and how to live it. Nothing pleases them more than when someone comes to understand the Bible better. Teachers enjoy studying Scripture and discovering new ways to make it clear to others. Teachers communicate God's truth in formal and casual situations alike. Many express the gift of teaching by leading Sunday School classes or accompanying groups on retreats.

Encouraging. Encouragers prompt people to believe in God and live for Him. Encouragers notice the good which God creates in people and helps them respond to it. With the goal of motivating people to live as God wants them to, encouragers lovingly correct them and share edifying words. An encourager would be a definite asset to a church's nominating committee (the group who enlists Bible study teachers and fills other ministry needs).

Contributing to the needs of others. Givers notice and meet people's physical, emotional, and spiritual needs. Rather than feeling put out, they see giving as a way to serve God. Givers are often the first to offer services or ideas, frequently give in excess of a tithe, and often spend their time to help somebody else.

Leadership. Leaders guide both individuals and groups to obey God. They can motivate others without being pushy. They do so by helping the group see the good of an idea and find ways to make it reality. Leaders also guide each person to contribute his or her abilities to the endeavor. These individuals are humble because they too follow a leader, God Himself. A leader might be highly visible, or lead from a less obvious position.

Showing mercy. A merciful person feels the pain of others and seeks to relieve it. She notices the need behind another person's action and empathizes with her. A merciful person would visit someone in the hospital, invite a lonely person to lunch, take up for someone who's being criticized, or show tenderness rather than toughness.

Discover Your Gift
In order to discover your spiritual gift(s), notice what you already do well and how God might be using those abilities. Talk with God and trusted Christian friends about what your gift(s) might be. Consider these questions: (a) What do I like to do? (b) What do I do well? (c) What will benefit the church? (d) What does God want me to do? Throughout this process, continually ask God how you can use your gift(s) daily. Record your discoveries and conclusions:

I can show my spiritual gift(s) at church by . . .

I can show my spiritual gift(s) at home by . . .

I can show my spiritual gift(s) in my career (or in the way I spend most of my time) by . . .

Discover and use your gift(s) to bring unity to your church and glory to God.

🕊 *LIVE GOD'S WORD* 🕊

1. Memorize Romans 12:1-2. As you go through the day, deliberately give each word, action, and attitude to God—include washing dishes, talking with your family, driving, taking a shower—everything you do. How would you do these differently if you offered them to God? Notice the ways these "little" things go together to form a glorious day for God and His people.

2. Romans 11:33-36 is a "doxology," a song of praise to God. Write your own song of praise to God. Your tune can be a familiar hymn, a commercial jingle, or a melody you compose. Sing it (at least to yourself) for a couple days. Add new verses as you notice things to praise God for.

3. Invite your pastor, staff minister, and other church leaders to tell you how they first discovered their spiritual gifts and how God led them to develop these gifts. Be certain to include less visible leaders (see 1 Cor. 12:22) and ministers, such as nursery helpers, kitchen crew members, and encouragers.

4. When you notice individuals practicing prophesy, service, teaching, encouragement, giving, leadership, or mercy, tell them what you see. Doing so will certainly encourage them, and may help them discover their God-given gifts.

CHAPTER NINE

FROM ROMANCE TO *True Love*

🎵 *LISTEN TO GOD'S WORD* 🎵

Spending an evening with a romance novel (Christian, of course) can make me feel warm and gushy inside. It can also make me feel frustrated with the job pressures, the stacked-up laundry, and the constantly cluttered house I live with from day to day. Those things aren't part of the romance novels; and if they are, a kiss and a hug take care of them. Why can't life be like the novels, where people live happily ever after? Because God knows about something better—a love that runs deeper than the romances, a love that solves real life problems, a love that lasts longer and satisfies more thoroughly. This love is based in choices and commitments. Find freedom to discover and live true love in Romans 12:9-21.

Read Romans 12:9-21.
1. The word translated "sincere" in verse 9 literally means "without hypocrisy." Name three words that describe sincere love and three words that describe insincere love.
               SINCERE   INSINCERE

2. Do you find it easier to hate what is evil or cling to what is good? Why? Is it possible to do one without doing the other?

3. Why is other-centeredness the first quality in true love? (See v. 10.)

Name a time when someone loved you the way they wanted to love rather than the way you needed to be loved. What was your reaction?

4. Zeal is enthusiasm for serving God. It doesn't mean that you have to be worked-up or emotional, but that your commitment to please God stays paramount. Zeal is the opposite of trying to get by with as little work or inconvenience as possible. Spiritual fervor means you allow the Holy Spirit to set you on fire. When you have zeal and spiritual fervor, you serve God and others in His name, even if great energy is required. Describe someone who loves with the zeal of the Lord (see v. 11).

When have you loved with God's zeal?

5. Which comes first—joy in hope, patience in affliction, or faithfulness in prayer? (See v. 12.) Why?

6. Meeting another's genuine need is an honor, not a burden (see v. 13). Why?

Verse 13 encourages you to provide generously for the needs of fellow Christians and to practice hospitality. Hospitality requires opening your home and heart to others, giving someone a place to stay, or helping people feel at home. How do you do this for your own family? Your friends? Someone you don't know well?

Is hospitality limited to your home? Why or why not?

7. To bless and curse involve actions as well as words. How? (See v. 14.)

Name the words and actions you would use to bless someone who persecutes you. How would these help solve the problem between you and your persecutor?

8. Do you find it easier to rejoice with someone or mourn with her? To find someone to rejoice with you or mourn with you? (See v. 15.)

It can be hard to find a Christian who will walk through sorrow (mourn) with you because many Christians want to explain away the pain or say that nothing is the matter. They find pain contrary to faith. Why is it OK for the Christian to experience sadness? (See also Ecc. 3:4.)

9. Harmony exists when people who are different have a common mind. How does humility enhance harmony? (See v. 16.) How does willingness to associate with all persons enhance it? How do you practice these attitudes?

Verse 16 names pride and conceit as attitudes counterproductive to harmony. Give examples of actions that demonstrate these attitudes.

What other attitudes make it hard to live in harmony with others?

10. Because the world watches how Christians live, Christians must not choose actions that discredit the faith. How could repaying evil for evil discredit Christianity? (See v. 17.)

Refusing to repay evil for evil does not mean to passively do nothing. Instead, it means to choose another path—a path that is more obviously "right in the eyes of everybody" (12:17). Name an evil and a path that would stop that evil more effectively than retaliation (see Matt. 18:15-20).

11. Name a situation in which you worked unsuccessfully for peace. Why is it important to work toward peace even if you don't achieve it? (See Rom. 12:18; Matt. 5:9.)

When someone refuses our efforts toward peace or responds with further alienation, it hurts. We may want to retaliate. However, God can give us peace even if the other party refuses peace. How?

12. Tell about a time you were tempted to take revenge (see v. 19).

In the situation above, why would the actions in verse 20 work toward peace better than taking revenge?

Only God has enough insight to make the punishment fit the crime. Why? What else makes Him the only one qualified to avenge?

13. Name some evils you currently face. What good actions could overcome them? (See v. 21.) Start with examples of these.

Greed:

Gossip:

Manipulation:

Selfishness:

Destructive anger:

Note that God Himself has chosen to overcome evil with good, redemption being the prime example. Name others.

14. Will the love actions in Romans 12:9-21 really work? Romans 15:1-7 explains that Jesus chose to love others rather than please Himself, and it worked. As you read the verses below, notice how Jesus loved and how you could love the same ways:

THE ACTION	HOW JESUS DID IT	HOW I CAN DO IT
Please neighbor for his good (see 15:1-4)		
Receive God's spirit of unity (see vv. 5-6)		
Accept each other (see v. 7)		

15. Love verses like those in Romans 12 and 15 can make us yearn to be loved in this way. What characteristics of love do you most yearn for in your marriage? Your friendships? Your church relationships? (see 12:9-21; 15:1-7)

Since *your* actions are the only ones you can change and because quality loving invites quality loving in return, focus on your own love actions. Write each love action from Romans 12:9-21. Behind each, add the name or initials of a person you need to love with that action. Talk with God about opportunities to do so.

LOVE ACTION	PERSON TO LOVE WITH THIS ACTION

For Further Study
Examine 1 Corinthians 13:4-7. How does it enhance your understanding of Romans 12:9-21 and 15:1-7?

LIFE EXAMPLE:
❦ Why Love Works Better Than Romance ❦

Ultimately, love is a series of choices — the choice to bring good and not evil to people with our words and actions. We choose to create unity rather than alienation. We choose to work conflicts out directly rather than get back slyly. We choose to find the best route rather than the one that "feels right." We choose to care rather than to keep score. Choosing to love is initially harder but can bring deeper loyalty than romance.

Romance, on the other hand, is a feeling. It's the gushy feeling you get when someone handsome walks into the room. It's wanting your husband to tell you he can't live without you — that if you hadn't come along when you did, he'd have searched for you forever. It's the agony of anticipation and wondering if the hero and heroine will get together. Romance ends with "They lived happily ever after." Love then is making that "happily ever after" happen. Romance is not bad — it's just not enough. It can't get you through the stomach flu or lack of money or worse. Love, on the other hand, can transform routine into joy and can demonstrate lifelong commitment.

Practice God's love principles by imagining yourself in each situation below. How could each love action from Romans 12:9-21 help you create love rather than pain? The first has been done as a sample.

Love Situation A. You and your children have been squabbling frequently. Your fatigue and their repeated winter illnesses have contributed to this problem. How could actions like not being lacking in zeal, being joyful in hope, and overcoming evil with good help this matter?

Solution: Because zeal is enthusiasm for serving God (even when it means work or inconvenience), I will depend on the Holy Spirit for strength. I can use this zeal to meet my children's needs during both sick and well intervals (driving to doctors vs. driving to school events; taking temperatures and giving medicines vs. giving practice drills). I'll add interest to their days with interesting crafts and games. When my children are more occupied, they'll be less fussy and I'll be less irritable.

I can be joyful in hope, knowing that winter illnesses usually don't last through the spring. Maybe I can appreciate the closed-in time with my children by realizing that we'd be running like crazy if they were well. I can be joyful in hope with the continuing challenges of my daughter's hearing loss, knowing that in heaven she won't have these struggles.

Because illnesses and chronic frustrations are the devil's doing, I can overcome his evil efforts with creativity, innovation, and persistence. I can be creative by letting my children draw or listen to music when they are too sick to read. I can be innovative by getting sleep here and there rather than staying fatigued and irritable. I can be persistent by understanding and equipping my hearing-impaired daughter, no matter how great the frustrations grow. I can find power to do this by remembering that God is always stronger than evil.

In addition to choosing to love my children in these ways, I can choose to tell them why I'm irritable. When they understand, they won't feel that I'm personally attacking them; they may even minister to my needs.

Love Situation B. Rumors have been spread about you at church. The person who spread them is a friend who turned on you in a moment of anger. How could attitudes like sincerity, honoring of each other, and patience solve this sticky situation? What words would you use to express these attitudes to your friend? To others who heard the rumors?

Love Situation C. You and your spouse stay so busy with work, church, and parenting that you have little time for each other. You love to be together but have little energy to enjoy each other when you *do* get to be alone. How could actions like devotion, rejoicing and mourning with each other, and being careful to do what is right help?

Love Situation D. Members of your church are taking opposite sides on a church decision. You yearn for unity (see Rom. 15:5) but don't see how it can come about when each side is convinced that its opinion is God's will. How could actions like sharing, hospitality, being faithful in prayer, and refusing to seek revenge help?

Love Situation E. Your parent criticizes you and your children. Since your parent treats everyone that way, you shouldn't take it personally, but you do. How could leaving room for God's wrath, giving food and drink to your enemy, and overcoming evil with good bring love?

Jesus' solutions are difficult but definite. See how He leads you through rough relationships. Choose to love. As you choose to follow God's guidance in your loving, you'll create closeness, solve problems, and find lasting joy. You'll learn that love is better than romance.

❧ LIVE GOD'S WORD ❧

1. Memorize Romans 12:21. Every time you face an evil situation this week, jot in your journal good actions or attitudes that could overcome the evil. Invite God to communicate with you through the writing process.

2. There are over 20 love actions in Romans 12:9-21. Write one on each day of this month's calendar. When you run out of love actions, repeat the ones you especially want to work on. Look at your calendar every day and focus on doing the designated love action for that day.

3. If you do calligraphy, cross-stitch, or other letter art, create a poster with part or all of Romans 12:9-21. Consider making a second poster for a young person who is dating or waiting to date. Many young people are amazed to find such powerful love advice in the Bible.

4. We often label love a feeling rather than a choice. Letting feelings direct our love can be dangerous because they can deceive us. For example, name a time when you acted out of false guilt rather than love. Or, name a time when you did something out of false confidence instead of love.

FROM ROUGH *Relationships* TO SMOOTH

CHAPTER TEN

❧ LISTEN TO GOD'S WORD ❧

Rough relationships can make Christlike love more difficult to show. Some of these rough relationships are in the workplace or the community—a boss who drives you crazy or a local official who does a not-so-great job. You encounter other rough relationships at church—a gripy committee member or a deacon who throws a tantrum when he doesn't get his way. Still other rough relationships meet you in your own home—a child you find hard to talk with or a family member with a temper. Find freedom to love your way through rough relationships as you study Romans 13–14.

Read Romans 13:1–14:19.

1. Do you think "authorities" refers to the office or to the people in those offices? (See 13:1-7.) Why?

   Are the people in office always there because it is God's will? Notice that Mark 13:9-11 foretells of persons opposed to God in government positions. What difference would it make if the positions of authority were established by God but not the specific persons in the positions?

2. Give an example of submitting to a governing authority in your life (see Rom. 13:1-2). What good resulted?

Give an example of rebelling against a governing authority. Can good come from this? Does God ever approve of such rebellion?

Now respond to these examples.

☐ America was founded by colonists who revolted against their homeland authorities. Do you think this pleased or offended God?

☐ Hitler killed millions of people during his rule and pulled the world into war. A Christian named Dietrich Bonhoeffer felt led by God to participate in a plan to assassinate Hitler. Hitler's people arrested and executed Bonhoeffer before he could carry out the plan. Could Bonhoeffer have prevented the killing of so many people? Does God approve of our working against authority figures who work against Him?

3. When and why do you fear authorities? How does doing right take away your fear? (See 13:3-5.)

Describe an authority who lives the truths in verses 3-6.

4. Which do you find easiest to pay to those who govern you: taxes, respect, or honor? (See vv. 6-7.) Hardest? Why?

5. During most of Paul's ministry, Roman emperors protected freedom of worship. Later, emperors such as Nero vengefully tortured and murdered Christians. How should Christians obey verses 1-5 in light of this? In light of present government?

Review the principles of Christian love in 12:9-21. How do these impact the way you relate to authority figures as addressed in 13:1-7?

6. Romans 13:1-7 speaks of the Christian's responsibilities to governing authorities. The rest of the chapter describes the Christian's obligations to other people. As you read verses 8-14, focus on the relationships in your home and extended family. What one debt do we owe to all our fellow Christians? (See vv. 8-9.) Why can it never be fully paid?

7. Name several specific actions from verses 9-14 that fulfill God's command to love. Notice that some actions are stated negatively, such as, "Do not commit adultery." State these positively; for example: "Be faithful to my spouse" or "Remain sexually pure as a single." In the third column suggest a way your doing each would create closeness in your family.

LOVE ACTION   POSITIVE TRANSLATION   HOW IT CREATES
                                         CLOSENESS

8. When family relationships get rough, members start to keep score. What does verse 8 say about this?

Remembering that love is a choice (not just something you do when you feel positively toward someone), tell how well you fulfill your debt of love to each of your family members.

9. Notice Paul's metaphors of sleeping and waking, night and day, darkness and light in verses 11-12. These metaphors convey the good news that salvation is close and the bad news that we have limited time. How do you love your family members in the light of the culmination of our salvation? In the light of limited time?

Many loving actions go undone simply because we neglect to do them. What love needs do you miss? Which ones are you awake to? (See vv. 11-14.)

To clothe means to take off some items and put on others. Describe what it means to "clothe yourselves with the Lord Jesus Christ" (v. 14) regarding your family.

10. Shift your love focus one more time to difficult relationships in your church. Paul addressed two groups who were threatening the unity of the church by wrangling over issues that were not matters of salvation. What were these issues, according to Romans 14:1-19?

How can you tell the difference between a "matter of eating and drinking" and a true question of faith ("righteousness, peace, and joy in the Holy Spirit")? (v. 17; also see vv. 5-8)

11. The weak Christians needed rules and regulations to obey God. The strong Christians understood the principle behind the rules and were able to obey God without the specific rules. How can these two groups find unity in the same church? (See vv. 1-8; and 1 Cor. 8–9.)

Does unity mean agreement? Uniformity? Why or why not? How does understanding the other's point of view help smooth out divisions?

How does the fact of 14:9 impact disagreements between Christians?

12. To whom are we ultimately responsible? (See vv. 7-12.) How does this knowledge ease your need to:

Judge other Christians—

Condemn them—

Correct them—

Insist that other believers see things your way—

Establish power—

13. Rather than judging, condemning, correcting, insisting, and establishing power, we Christians can love and teach one another. What's the difference between not putting "any stumbling block or obstacle" in a fellow Christian's way and giving someone her own way simply because she wants it? (See vv. 13-18.)

The "weak" tended to insist on legalism and were critical of those who didn't observe their rules. How can the weak teach the strong about rules without taking away the freedom of the strong in Christ? (See vv. 13-19.)

The strong tended to look down on those who focused on rules rather than on Jesus and His intention for those rules. How can a strong Christian teach a weak one about a biblical idea that has not previously matched the weak one's set of rules?

14. Notice the phrases in verse 19: "do what leads to peace" and "to mutual edification." To edify is to build up, encourage, strengthen, and unify for Christ's sake. The way that initially looks peaceful is not always the edifying way. Tell why.

What specific actions would bring both the peace and the edification your church needs? (See 14:17, 19.) Which does God want you to take?

15. Review the ten chapters in this book and the struggles they address. Choose the one closest to your current experience and jot down at least two actions or truths that can equip you to manage and triumph in the midst of your struggle. Write a Bible verse or verse portion to go with each.

For Further Study
1. Reread the entire Book of Romans in one sitting. Notice the truths that jump out at you as a result of your recent study. Recall that Romans is a powerful overview of life's important questions: *Why are we here? What does God want from us? How do we relate to God? To other Christians? What do problems mean? What does the future hold?*
2. Read Romans one final time (one chapter a day) and notice the questions it answers. Choose a specific promise to live each day.

LIFE EXAMPLE:
❧ The Importance of Not Knowing It All ❧

I assume that I'm right. If I celebrate a holiday, I think everyone else should enjoy it too. If I skip a holiday, dissatisfied with its pagan origins, I prefer that others skip it too. When I discipline or care for my children in a particular way, I think I'm doing the right thing. I feel strongly about how church should happen and why. I want to work for God's kingdom, and want other Christians to join me.

Some people call this being opinionated. Some call it having convictions. What I do with my ideas is also important. I can be a cooperative member of the body of Christ, deferring my opinions in favor of God's directions; or I can declare I'm right and insist that others agree. I can quietly live out my convictions, respectfully sharing the how's and why's of my choices; or I can campaign for people to join my side. I can learn from other people's choices, noticing the many facets of good; or I can insist my idea is the only valid one. Obviously, the first of each pair is better. I pray I'll listen to the Holy Spirit's continual prompting to "do what leads to peace and to mutual edification" (Rom. 14:19).

I'm not the only one struggling with this problem. From Herod to Hitler, people have assumed their way, and only their way, is right. They fuss, bicker, demand, use, and distrust anyone who wants to do things differently. These people create divisions ranging in size from two-person power struggles to worldwide wars. Some have found homes in our churches and assume they are acting on God's behalf.

Neither I nor any other one person know it all. That's important because it makes me receptive to learning from others in my church and home. It opens me to understanding new truths about God that I never would have seen from my stage or position in life. It frees me to enjoy unity. Since I can trust other people, I don't have to try to control every action and attitude in my home, church, and community.

Accepting that I don't know it all fosters love because it gives other people the opportunity to teach me, love me, and help me grow. It motivates me to love others by understanding why they do things differently and how God is guiding them in that path. It guides me to love God because I can stop judging and start trusting Him.

I don't know it all. It's risky because I might trust someone who's not trustworthy. I might be used by someone who thinks he or she knows it all and has to prove it. The risks grow small as I use what I do know to evaluate people and ideas. The risks shrink further when I pray that God will guide my church and me in the paths He has set for us, not in human-made paths.

The same determined drive that gives me convictions empowers me to choose to love and respect people, especially my brothers and sisters in Christ. I determine to follow God's guidance in relationships, no matter how hard it is on me personally. I determine to find loving actions that bring good to my church and community.

I don't know it all, but I know the One who does and that:
- ☐ authorities have been established by God (see Rom. 13:1);
- ☐ "rulers hold no terror for those who do right" (v. 3);
- ☐ I must pay taxes, revenue, respect, and honor (v. 7);
- ☐ I have a continuing debt to love other people (v. 8);
- ☐ my love must do no harm to my neighbor (v. 10);
- ☐ I live to the Lord and die to the Lord, accountable to Him like everyone else for all my actions and attitudes (14:8, 12);
- ☐ "every tongue will confess to God" (v. 11);
- ☐ I must not put a stumbling block in front of someone else (v. 13);
- ☐ I must work toward peace and mutual edification (v. 19).

You've come to the end of your study of Romans. Rather than stopping here, let God's truths from the Book of Romans continue to transform your life. Rather than feel guilty for or controlled by your struggles, let God help you understand them and discover what to do about them. Sometimes this will mean turning the struggle into a catalyst for deeper spiritual growth—for example, a fight with a friend leads you to discover how to communicate more clearly. At other times, the frustration will provide opportunity for a firmer expression of faith—for instance, a battle with a bad habit leads you to develop the courage to change. At still other times, the frustration means leaning on God's everlasting arms—in this case, God compassionately walks with you through a tragic death to weep with you, to empower you to face the challenges ahead, to hold you, and to assure you of His steady care. Based on passages in Romans, discover how God will equip you to find Christ's freedom in the midst of your particular struggles. With God's help, you can learn the cause of your struggle, address it according to His direction, and move toward freedom in Christ.

❧ LIVE GOD'S WORD ❧

1. Memorize Romans 14:17-19. Write it word for word in your journal and list specific ways you have seen people carry out this verse. Keep adding examples until you have at least 20. Circle those you want to imitate.
2. Recall someone who loved you when you were not easy to love. Remember the good this love brought out in you. Thank God for loving you through this person. Telephone or write that person to express your thanks.
3. Ponder God's steady love for you. Create a symbol or write a song, a poem, or a saying of thanks for His love. How does His love motivate you to love others?
4. Write out your favorite verse from the Book of Romans. Post it on your bathroom mirror or the dashboard of your car until you have memorized it. Live its truth.
5. Love a hard-to-love person with the principles in Romans 13–14. Remember that loving actions frequently come before loving feelings. Choose a verse such as 13:8 or 14:19 as your motivation. Consider covenanting with a trusted friend to love the same hard-to-love person.

♊ LEADER'S GUIDE ♊

As you lead the study, emphasize that since God speaks to us through His Word, we should listen to Him through His Word. Encourage members of your group to do this rather than depend too much on Bible commentaries or human teachers. Urge the members to complete the *Listen to God's Word* section prior to each meeting. This systematic inductive study will help keep group discussion biblically based.

In each chapter, you will lead the group in discussing select (but not all) study questions from *Listen to God's Word*. Supplement the discussion of select questions with the information found in the *Group Participation* section of the leader's guide.

Though this study is based on the *New International Version*, take advantage of the different versions that might be brought to the meeting. Or make it a point to bring and use various translations. Explain that the Bibles we have today are English translations of the original Greek writings. Because Greek is a much more precise language, *exact* translation into English is difficult. As a fortunate result, translators choose a variety of ways to express Bible truth—a variety which can enhance our understanding of God's Word.

Allow time near the end of the meeting to interact with the narrative section *(Life Example)* and the application exercises *(Live God's Word)*. Invite members to share their responses. There's great potential in this for encouraging each other to live God's way. Suggest that telling others about our decisions can make us accountable to them to follow through with our plans—the very motivation that many of us need. Finally, encourage members to share the successes and achievements they've had applying lessons from the meetings.

❧ LEADER'S GUIDE 1 ❧

Objective
To discover that beliefs always affect actions.

Personal Preparation
1. Let the words of Romans 1:16-32 speak to and convict you. Refuse to use the passage like a club with which to attack others.
2. Ponder the many ways God has revealed Himself to you.

Group Time
☐ Introduce yourself. Invite group members to get acquainted by stating their names, favorite Bible verse, and why they love it.
☐ **Question 1** Point out that the Gospel is centered in Jesus Christ, who is God's Son and our Lord. Ask: **What is the Gospel? What qualifies Jesus to save us?** Supplement by adding to the discussion that He is uniquely qualified to save us and create righteousness in us because (a) He is both God and human, (b) because God raised Him from death, (c) because He fulfills the promises God made before His coming, and (d) because God sent Him to save. Encourage members to notice descriptions of the Gospel throughout the Book of Romans.
☐ **Question 2** Explain that the Prophet Habakkuk asked God, in the Bible book Habakkuk, why evil men seem to triumph. God responded by encouraging a faithful lifestyle in the midst of evil. Good guys may finish last, but they're the only ones who finish (Hab. 2:4).
☐ **Question 3** Point out that accepting God means to live in obedience to His lordship, not just to recognize His existence. Those who reject God are guilty not because they misunderstand Him, but because they willfully reject Him and show that rejection in their actions.
☐ **Question 4** Explain that though God's wrath is a natural result of human choices, it is also anger. Unlike human anger, God's anger is designed to draw us toward repentance. The wrath we experience now is a foretaste of what will come at the last judgment. Discuss wrath further by asking:

  ☐ *Is everything that happens a product of our choices?*
  ☐ *When are we to blame for our circumstances? When are others to blame?*
  ☐ *When is no one to blame?*

☐ **Question 5** Note that God is the one who tells about Himself through nature. Nature itself is not the speaker.

☐ **Question 6** Explain that the heart (see Rom. 1:21) was seen as the organ of thought, will, and decision, not feeling. As always, the heart's choices aren't necessarily good.

☐ **Question 7** Point out that when a person rejects God, she condemns herself to an inferior standard of life for at least one of these reasons: (a) she arrogantly chooses to be her own god; (b) she chooses idolatry by making someone or something less than God to be her god; (c) she distorts relationships by accepting inferior standards for love; (d) she cruelly determines that anything is OK if it benefits the person rejecting God. These points are all illusions of happiness that bring confusion rather than contentment.

☐ **Question 9** Explain that problems with sexuality are not new. During Paul's day, pagans worshiped their gods and goddesses by having sex with temple prostitutes. Meanwhile, the Jews loathed homosexual practices and wouldn't tolerate them. Paul explained that homosexuality and other sexual sins pervert God's good gift. Homosexuality is contrary to God's created order and brings negative consequences (for instance, less-than-happy relationships, the extinction of the human race). Similarly, heterosexual practices without a loving marriage union hurt people rather than draw them closer.

☐ **Question 10** Point out that without God to guide it, the mind can cause great problems. When people deny God, they cannot know themselves or be capable of rational thought. When people reject God, they reject their own minds, in a sense.

☐ **Question 12** Extend the discussion by asking:
  ☐ *Is it possible to be happy without God?*
  ☐ *Can humans create good?*
  ☐ *What potential do people have to make it on their own?*

☐ **Question 13** Guide members to notice how their beliefs affect their actions. Use these discussion starters from the passage:
  ☐ *How do you show you are not ashamed of the Gospel?*
  ☐ *How do you teach truth rather than suppress it?*
  ☐ *How do you honor God with your ideas? With the things you value? With your sexual practices? With the way you treat people?*

❧ LEADER'S GUIDE 2 ❧

Objective
To see that faith is not defined by trappings but by heart obedience.

Personal Preparation
1. As you read Romans 2:1-29, underline promises that impact your life. Remember to observe your own behavior, not someone else's.
2. Romans 1 describes the lostness and depravity of a secular or pagan society as it chose to live without God. Romans 2 describes persons who are concerned with religious things yet remain unrepentant. Prepare for learning by naming ways you are like these two parties.

Group Time
☐ **Question 1** Explain that Paul addressed the heathen in Romans 1 and the Jews in Romans 2. The Jews approved of God's judgment on the pagans, assuming their status made them judgment-proof. Ask:
  ☐ *Why was this assumption incorrect?*
  ☐ *How are many churchgoers like the Jews in their attitude?*
Point out that the phrase "do the same things" in Romans 2:1 refers to committing the essence of a sin, not necessarily the very same action. While the Jews would never accept homosexual expression or any of the other sins in chapter 1, they did commit the same essential sin—ignoring God.
☐ **Question 6** Point out the word "persistence" in verse 7. Ask:
  ☐ *When do you need persistence in seeking glory, honor, and immortality?*
  ☐ *Why is self-seeking so appealing?*
Caution members against concluding they must do good to earn God's love. Emphasize that our salvation is secure in Jesus Christ and is not the reward for good actions. Ask: **What's the difference between serving God because you love Him and serving Him to earn His love?**
☐ **Question 7** Point out that believing you have privileged status can lead you to think God will overlook certain wrongs. This error is based in the myth that God likes "religious" people better. Though the Jews believed they were God's chosen people, they weren't behaving like it. They seemed to expect God to do their will rather than vice versa. Believers are safe, but not immune from correction. Our Christian position should make us teachable, give us the security to obey out of love rather than obligation, make us aware of our responsibility to do right, and motivate us to fulfill it.

☐ **Question 8** Invite group response to the excuse, "I don't understand the Bible well enough to obey God." Encourage members to start obeying what they *do* know of the Bible, even as they continue to learn. Share how you plan to do so.

Explain that at the time Romans was written, the Jews had a rich heritage and more of God's revelation than the rest of the world; but these things resulted in no advantage because many Jews did not use them. Today, we enjoy the entire Bible—Old and New Testaments.

☐ **Question 10** Ideally, we ought to understand right and wrong simply because we are created by God. But experiences, such as "getting away with sin," can skew this. A growing relationship with God which is guided by the Bible can keep the conscience tender and responsive.

☐ **Question 12** Explain that Jews were proud of their identity as a people. They relied on their strict obedience to the Law to give them a secure position with God. But justification takes place first and expresses itself in obedience second, not vice versa. Paul used rhetorical questions to remind the proud Jews of the importance of practicing what they preached. The people's specific sins varied, but the essential sin was the same—rebellion against God.

☐ **Question 13** Circumcision, the ritual removal of the male foreskin, is only as valuable as the attitude that accompanies the rite. This ceremony no more makes one acceptable before God than church attendance makes one Christian. Paul did not discount circumcision but rather tried to show its relationship to devotion. An uncircumcised Gentile who demonstrates righteousness with God will be counted as circumcised, as a full member of God's family (2:26). Ask the members for outward signs often equated with devotion to God.

☐ **Question 15** Explain that we can encourage and motivate others to grow by sharing with them the effects of their actions or attitudes. If we practice this humbly, it keeps us from destructive relationships, helps us decide how to minister, and enables us to discover ways to solve conflicts.

Discuss 2:28-29 by explaining that the word "Jew" translates a Hebrew word meaning "praise." Thus a true Jew is praised by God, not any human standard. Ask:

☐ *How do you suppose the Jews felt after hearing Romans 2?*
☐ *What lifestyle changes do you think they made?*
☐ *What changes will you make in order to become praise to God and to be praised by God?*

🍂 LEADER'S GUIDE 3 🍂

Objective
To discover that the security and motivation offered by a relationship with Jesus Christ as Lord are superior to the pressure to please.

Personal Preparation
As you read Romans 3:9-31, note the love expressed by God even in the midst of our sinfulness. Ponder the initial and daily response this invites. As you read 4:1-25 notice that you are a child of Abraham. Thank God for including you in His family when you responded to Him in faith.

Group Time
☐ **Question 1** Stress that because every person, whether churched or unchurched, is under the power of sin, we all begin the same: enslaved by sin and needing Jesus to free or redeem us. Explain that 3:10-18 is a series of Old Testament quotes that explain why religiousness is not enough to merit acceptance before God. These quotes are: Psalm 14:1-3 (vv. 10-12); Psalms 5:9 and 140:3 (v. 13); Psalm 10:7 (v. 14); Isaiah 59:7-8 (vv. 15-17); and Psalm 36:1 (v. 18). Invite readings from various translations. One must fear or honor God before following His law works and before justification can take place (see v. 18).
☐ **Question 2** "The glory of God" (3:23) is what God intended all people to find. Because no one is good enough for God, He shows the way He has provided for righteousness—a way of relationship, a way of faith.
☐ **Question 4** Point out that God lovingly gave Himself to justify us. Avoid the conclusion that God angrily attacked His Son for the sake of justice, for God and His Son are one. Avoid too the conclusion that God is indifferent to sin; for He does all He can to eradicate it, including giving the Law, dying for us, and now encouraging our faith to help us not sin. Explain that when God justifies people, He declares them righteous and not guilty, and cancels the guilt of their sin. His love and justice go hand in hand. If this were not so, justice without love would mean annihilation; and love without justice would mean indifference to sin and its effects.
☐ **Question 5** Point out that people will more readily take action for a relationship than for a principle. Ask why. Invite members to share from *Life Example*. Then explain that the relationship brings out the elements of trust, love, and confidence. Suggest that faith points us

toward God's way of living and the Law shows us how. Ask members why faith motivates them to follow ("uphold," 3:31) the Law.

☐ **Question 7** Emphasize that a true child of Abraham (one accepted by God) is not necessarily a physical descendant of his, but one who expresses faith as Abraham did (4:13). Supplement with these highlights: Abraham's offspring are "all who believe" (v. 11) and who "walk in . . . faith" (v. 12). "The righteousness that comes by faith" (v. 13) brings the promise, not the Law. (This is significant because Jews had great confidence in the Law.) Faith and the promise are worthless if "those who live by the Law are heirs" (v. 14). "The promise comes by faith" (v. 16), so Jews and non-Jews alike who live by faith are Abraham's offspring. Abraham's faith was credited to him as righteousness 14 years before he was circumcised.

Circumcision was a seal of righteousness, not the cause of it (see vv. 9-11). People's belief makes them Abraham's descendants, not circumcision (v. 11). The circumcised are also descendants of Abraham if they walk in faith.

Suggest that churched people today are similar to the Jews of Paul's day if they feel secure in their "holy position." Churchgoers also tend to rank others by church service, obedience, and background. Ask the group what message God might want to give believers about righteousness and relationship with Him.

☐ **Question 8** Explain that whereas faith is a response to God, religion is the attempt to get God to respond to us.

☐ **Question 12** Note that a loving relationship encourages response: we care for and do for people we love. A relationship with God enables us to trust Him, believe Him, and obey Him. Encourage examples by asking:

☐ *How do you show your friends you love them?*
☐ *How do you show God you love Him?*

❧ LEADER'S GUIDE 4 ❧

Objective
To discover that God is working to redeem sin in all its expressions.

Personal Preparation
Romans 5:1-21 is full of theological words and concepts, such as *glorified, grace, righteous*, and others. Underline these words as you read. Study them with a concordance and a Bible dictionary. Use your study to supplement discussion of these words and concepts.

Group Time
☐ **Question 2** Supplement discussion of "access" as needed with: "Access" in 5:2 means an introduction into the presence of someone exalted. Prior to Christ, only the high priest could come directly into the presence of God. No longer must believers stand outside the holiest place to wait for the services of a priest. See Ephesians 2:18 and 3:12 in the *King James Version* for other uses of "access."

Grace is God's full acceptance of us apart from our performance. Grace is God seeing you as you *can be* rather than how you *are*. Grace provides a secure place to stand because it is based on God's love. Above all, grace is a free gift to us.

"The hope of the glory of God" (Rom. 5:2) may be the divine splendor that Adam lost in the Fall and which we anticipate recovering on the last day. It may be a future goal that God intends for people in the age to come. Or the glory of God may be His ideal for people now—a presently attainable goal. In each case, it is the climax of justification.

☐ **Question 3** Suggest that "rejoice in [our] suffering" (5:3) might be better stated "rejoice in the midst of our suffering." Paul believed that suffering signaled the return of Jesus, which Paul considered the cause for rejoicing—not the suffering itself.

☐ **Question 4** Perseverance is not simply being able to get through problems, but it is regarding God as more powerful than problems; looking past the problem to see God. The Greek word is a compound one, including a noun that means "staying" and a preposition that means "under." Perseverance is the capacity to stay under a heavy load until it is lifted. Finally, perseverance (which expresses patience or endurance) is active rather than passive.

Character denotes more than moral worth; it means that which has been tested and approved. This word was used of metal whose impurities had been burned out by fire. A person of character has learned to look to God during trial and to rest securely on hope in Him.

Hope is not wishful thinking or guesswork, but confidence based in facts. "Hope does not disappoint us" because it is based in God (5:5).

☐ **Question 5** Caution members that it isn't only sad times that make us become like Jesus. God uses all occasions, happy and sad, so that we can be "conformed to the likeness of His Son" (Rom. 8:29). Becoming like Jesus in happy times is just as much a miracle as becoming like Him in sad times. For in happy times, it's easy to feel self-sufficient; and in sad times, it's easy to become bitter.

☐ **Question 7** Reconciliation restores a relationship (2 Cor. 5:18-19). People who choose to be reconciled spiritually choose to stop acting against God. Reconciliation and justification express similar truths; they put an end to enmity between God and each repentant sinner. They are also present actions that guarantee the future culmination of salvation.

☐ **Question 10** Explain that Adam and Jesus were exposed to similar temptations. But while Adam chose to rebel, Jesus chose to obey God. Today we face the same choices as they did. Note the difference between the results of sin and righteousness.

☐ **Question 12** Point out that sinners aren't those who do only bad but those who ignore or work against God. Likewise, the righteous aren't those who do only good, but those who are justified by, reconciled to, and giving honor to God.

❧ LEADER'S GUIDE 5 ❧

Objective
To make specific action commitments to change destructive habits to constructive ones, for the sake of Christ.

Personal Preparation
As you read Romans 6:1-14, jot in the margin a way that each phrase impacts a specific action or attitude in your life. Let God humble you and make you aware of your dependence on Him. Refuse to feel self-righteous or superior to your group members. Come to the meetings willing to grow together.

Group Time
☐ **Question 1** Explain that Romans 6 (especially the first verses) addresses the question of dying to sin and living to Christ. Suggest that the best motivation for being good is not the avoidance of punishment but the attractiveness of doing good. Doing good expresses one's trust in God and brings happiness to people. Ask: **Why does obeying God bring joy? Contentment? Security?**
☐ **Question 2** Some translations (such as the *King James Version*) render the last part of 6:4 as "Walk in newness of life." Explain that the Christian's walk is her lifestyle, her manner of living, her actions and attitudes. Grace enables her to walk more like Jesus.
☐ **Question 3** Explain that in New Testament times, baptism was the way converts made public their commitment to Jesus Christ as Savior and Lord. Baptism does not have saving power but rather demonstrates that salvation has occurred. Suggest that group members name in one word the reason for or result of their baptism. Examples: "obedience," "testimony," "commitment," and "declaration."
☐ **Question 4** Some Bible students see the "body of sin" (6:6) as all persons who have not accepted Jesus as Lord.
☐ **Question 9** State that no one intends to be an instrument of wickedness, but choosing not to avoid sin means choosing to serve wickedness. Invite members to share specific strategies for obeying 6:13.
☐ **Question 12** Encourage members to name habits that offend God, not merely ones that bother them. Review the last few paragraphs of *Life Example*, beginning at "Put the principles . . . " Challenge members to make themselves accountable to a friend regarding the changes God wants to make in them. Ask: **How would accountability help us more consistently offer ourselves to God?**

🐚 LEADER'S GUIDE 6 🐚

Objective
To find freedom from discouragement over sin so we can give God control.

Personal Preparation
1. As you read Romans 7:14–8:4, ponder an occasion you did something you didn't want to do, or didn't do something you *did* want to do. Invite God to give you compassion coupled with motivation to overcome sin.
2. Read through Romans 7–8, inviting God's perspective.

Group Time
☐ Begin by directing the group to read this passage responsively. Let members in Group 1 read the "good" part of every verse or construction. The members in Group 2 will read the "sinful" part. Divide 7:15 thus:

    Group 1—"I do not understand what I do. For what I want to do . . ."
    Group 2—". . . I do not do, but what I hate I do."

☐ **Question 1** Introduce the passage by explaining that Romans 7:14–8:4 depicts the Christian's battle with sin. Emphasize that sin is the culprit—not the good, God-given Law, which simply makes sin apparent.

    In some Bible versions (such as the *King James*), the word translated "unspiritual" (7:14) is translated "carnal." Both words mean "ruled by a force opposite to God." Conversely, "spiritual" means "originating with God." Refusing to yield to God results in the enslaving of oneself to someone or something else—in this case, frustration over sin.

☐ **Question 2** Invite members to define sin and tell why it is a problem. Explain that the Law cannot solve the sin problem but can make it apparent. Only Jesus Christ, through the Holy Spirit, can make us good. Jesus helps us obey the right and avoid wrong that the Law has shown us.

☐ **Question 4** Comment that, though we Christians are delivered from sin, our release is never so complete that we can stop battling the appeal of sin, or cease reminding ourselves of its destructiveness. We have put on Christ but will not totally take off our sin nature until we reach heaven. Knowing this is an important step to defeating sin.

☐ **Question 6** Note that people who turn to God before a situation becomes critical can save themselves a lot of pain. However, some people have to feel desperate before they realize their need for God. Ask: **Why would someone choose one approach or another?**

☐ **Question 8** Highlight that the law of sin brings only death and destruction. We are powerless to break its power. The law of the Spirit, though, brings life and breaks sin's dominion. While sin is strong, God's Spirit is stronger. Point out the condemnation of sin, not Christians, in 8:3.

☐ **Question 9** Highlight the powerful role the Holy Spirit plays in winning the battle with sin. Note that the Greek word for "spirit" occurs over 20 times in Romans 8, more than in any other chapter of Paul's letters. Invite members to share how the Holy Spirit has freed them from a specific sin.

☐ **Question 11** Encourage group members to close their eyes and ponder the love God expressed by His coming in human form to break the power of sin and to give us the Holy Spirit. Point out that rather than become angry with us, God acted on our behalf and gave us His power to solve the sin problem.

Suggest that the specific how-to's and why's of the Atonement (8:3-4) are not nearly as important as the love God expressed by achieving it. Explain that the Atonement is God's action to cover or cancel sin and to bring us back into harmony with His original intention for us. The "likeness of sinful man" (v. 3) does not mean Jesus was a sinner or that He only appeared to be a person. Instead, it means He was sent to earth and lived a real human life without sinning. God entered sin's realm (the flesh) and conquered it. We are now free to act in accordance with the Spirit, a freedom which the Law could not give.

❧ LEADER'S GUIDE 7 ❧

Objective
To recognize that pain is not contrary to faith.

Personal Preparation
1. As you read Romans 8:18-38, list the promises that impact your life.
2. Spend time praying for each group member, focusing on painful circumstances she may be facing.

Group Time
☐ **Question 1** If group members tend to decide that we should explain away or minimize suffering, change the direction of the conversation. Recall for the group Jesus' agony in the Garden of Gethsemane (Matt. 26:38-39; Luke 22:42-44). Point out that, while Paul suffered incredibly, he didn't bring it into his discourse in Romans. Some of his sufferings are described in 2 Corinthians 11:23–12:10.

☐ **Question 3** Nature, like people, is in bondage to sin and waits for redemption. Invite a member to read Genesis 3:17-19 as background for Romans 8:19-22. Note that creation's imperfections and groanings cannot be described as simple consequences of Adam's fall, because of the phrase "the will of the one who subjected it, in hope" (v. 20). Because of God, creation has hope. Note also that creation is under enslavement and that enslavement always corrupts. Creation will eventually be set free (see v. 21).

☐ **Question 5** Invite members to share how they feel about God ministering to them by praying for them. The "groans that words cannot express" (v. 26) may be unspoken or unspeakable. These groans come from the Spirit, who needs no words to communicate with God. The groans may also come from the Christian who, because of great emotion, can't put his or her needs into words. The Holy Spirit understands and communicates it to God the Father.

☐ **Question 6** Caution members against calling every event that happens the will of God, unless the Bible specifically declares it so. Tragedies are frequently caused by persons who choose to work against God's will, and in so doing inflict horrible pain on others. These occurrences are contrary to God's will and grievous to Him. He allows them for the sake of free will, but detests them. Other times tragedies or illnesses with no clear cause affect Christians. These make God as sad as they do us. So He offers His resources and power. Read 8:28 to make this clear. Ask: **When do we use Romans 8:28 as a pat answer? As a faith statement?**

☐ **Question 7** Invite each member to tell how the person on her left demonstrates "the likeness of His Son" (v. 29) with words, characteristics, and actions. In prayer, thank God for working in each person so precisely and personally.

While discussing the complicated terms in verses 29-30, emphasize that these verses are not a precise formula as much as a profound statement of faith that God has been working (and continues working) in human lives to bring us to Himself and His will. Note that foreknowledge and predestination are past; calling, justifying, and conforming are present; and glorification is future. Invite insight on the meanings of these actions, based on how other Scriptures use them (see concordance suggestion under *For Further Study*). Supplement with:

Foreknew. Literally, "knew beforehand." While God sees into the future and knows the choices people will make, He doesn't control these choices. Some say it's like watching a movie.

Be conformed to the likeness of His Son. To be made like Jesus. Jesus is not the only one who will share in a glorious future and the privileges of being a child of God—Christians will too. This will only fully be accomplished when we go to heaven.

Called. We are invited to follow Christ or appointed to serve God in a specific way or for a specific purpose. Those who respond to God's call help realize God's purposes. God takes the initiative to establish and build a relationship with us; then our response of obedience completes the calling.

Justified. Signifies that we are made right with God, given a status of righteousness by Him. He justifies those who respond in faith to His call. The righteousness brought by justification makes life, joy, and glorification possible.

Glorified. Fully conformed to Christ, which is the ultimate triumph of God's grace that will come at the end of the world. Glorification is so certain that Paul described it as though it had already happened.

☐ **Questions 8–9** Note that the only one with qualifications to condemn—namely, God—pleads our case instead. God has shown that He is for us by coming in the person of Jesus Christ to live, die, and rise from death. God has chosen, justified, and loved us thoroughly through Christ. Because He is for us, no dangers, problems, threats, or pains can threaten our salvation.

☐ **Question 11** Explain that many believed astrological powers controlled their destiny. "Height or depth" translate technical astronomical or astrological terms, meaning the highest point to which stars rise and lowest abyss.

🎵 LEADER'S GUIDE 8 🎵

Objective
To encourage members to discover and live their spiritual gifts.

Personal Preparation
1. As you read Romans 11:33-36, list why you want to serve God. Then, as you read Romans 12:1-5, list actions that would enable you to serve God better. As you read 12:6-8, record a spiritual gift you think God has given you with which to serve Him.
2. Ponder these two truths and plan to emphasize them as you lead: (a) God has given at least one gift to every Christian; and (b) gifts are to be used for the good of the church.

Group Time
☐ **Question 1** Some Bible notes identify 11:33-36 as a doxology. Explain that a doxology is a song of praise. Have members work in pairs to write songs of praise or share those they wrote for *Live God's Word.*

☐ **Question 3** Point out that offering ourselves to God produces sacrifices with these qualities: (a) living rather than dead (this could mean physically or spiritually alive); (b) holy rather than profane—we are dedicated to God rather than to self, another person, money, or any other cause; (c) pleasing to God rather than pleasing to another person or cause—God wants behavior, attitudes, and actions that please Him; (d) spiritual or reasonable, rather than unreasonable.

☐ **Question 6** Point out that pride must have been threatening the unity of the church, even as it does today. Perhaps this pride caused some people to think their spiritual gifts were more important than other people's spiritual gifts. The truth is that all Christians are equally important channels through whom God works, no matter how spectacular or commonplace the gifts seem. A biblical attitude toward self is important for expressing spiritual gifts. Why? A too-low self-esteem results in hesitance to use the gift God has given; and a too-high self-esteem results in self-exaltation or self-promotion rather than glorification of God.

☐ **Question 12** Define a career as the way a person spends his or her time. Discourage members from limiting the concept of career to conventional occupations (doctor, nurse, businesswoman). Encourage members to expand their thinking to include such options as mother and homemaker, ministry coordinator, and friendship evangelist.

❧ *LEADER'S GUIDE 9* ❧

Objective
To discover why God's loving actions work better than Hollywood's definition of love.

Personal Preparation
Read Romans 12:9-21. Next to each love action, pencil in the initials of (1) someone who loves you this way; and (2) someone you could love this way. Thank God for putting these people in your life.

Group Time
Because the word *love* tends to conjure up images of male-female romances, take care to expand loving relationships to include male-female friendships, boss-employee, fellow church members, neighbors, and other types of relationships.

☐ **Question 1** Ask group members how they can tell if someone's love is sincere or fake. Adjectives that describe sincere love include: concerned, other-centered, lasting through thick and thin, sacrificial. Adjectives that describe false love include manipulative, selfish, shallow, convenient. Ask: **Is it possible to be fooled by someone's love?**

☐ **Question 3** Ask someone to read Romans 12:10 from a RSV translation. Ask: **How can we "outdo one another in showing honor"?**

☐ **Question 7** Sample: Gossip can make people think less of the person talked about. This can lead to distrust or unfair treatment of that person. Invite members to name other cursing or blessing actions that grow from cursing or blessing words.

☐ **Question 10** C.K. Barrett describes a life that is "right in the eyes of everybody" (12:17) as one that an honest Greek would recognize as good (*The Epistle to the Romans*, p. 242). Discuss: **What is the difference between doing what is right in the eyes of everybody and giving in to peer pressure?**

☐ **Question 12** Explain that burning coals are the fire of remorse. The metaphor means that loving actions will bring remorse and repentance in one's enemy. The enemy may begin doing good.

   Agree that there are instances when God used or will use a human agent to execute His wrath, but only God can initiate and authorize these instances.

☐ **Question 15** Instruct group members to pray in pairs for each other: first, for the loving they need to receive; second, for the loving they need to give.

❧ LEADER'S GUIDE 10 ❧

Objective
To find freedom to love our way through frustrations.

Personal Preparation
1. As you read Romans 13:1–14:19, jot next to each principle words or actions that you could use to live out the principle.
2. Review the entire study guide, highlighting one point you want to emphasize from each session.

Group Time
☐ **Question 2** In Old Testament times, people were convinced that God was the ruler of all nations and protected His people with rulers. Paul probably wrote Romans between A.D. 54 and 58. To this point, there had been no official persecution of Christians in the Roman Empire. In A.D. 49, the Roman emperor Claudius expelled the Jews from Rome, possibly due to the disturbance created by the teaching that Jesus was the Christ. But in A.D. 54, Nero relaxed this edict and Jews returned to Rome. The actions Paul suggested in Romans 13 were given to avoid further problems. The government was able to protect Christians and provide an opportunity to share the good news of Jesus Christ. The Roman Christians may have needed special instructions in civic duties, perhaps because they were rebellious toward leaders or ignorant of their responsibilities. In addition to all this, Paul expected Jesus to return soon. Ask: **How do current government conditions impact how God wants us to understand Romans 13:1–14:19?**

☐ **Question 4** Authority figures deserve honor and respect not because they are important but because they are to serve God. Ask:
  ☐ *How is giving honor for God's sake easier than giving it for the official's sake?*
  ☐ *Why should Christians, like other citizens, obey their rulers?*

☐ **Questions 6–9** Some women are single, wives without children, women living with their mothers, divorcees, widows, friends living together, or some other grouping. So be certain to define family as the person(s) you live with or love.

☐ **Question 7** Approach this issue from another angle by asking: **How do you unintentionally commit adultery, murder, theft, and so on? Describe the damage these cause.** Suggest that a woman could as easily commit adultery by wishing she were married to someone else as she could by actually sleeping with another man. She could murder with words as well as with a weapon. She could steal objects or confidence. She could covet another person's job, situation, or looks.

☐ **Question 8** Suggest that when parties keep score, each feels that the other owes her an apology, a future concession, or a favor. Romans 13:8 focuses on our debt to others, not others' debt to us.

☐ **Question 11** Explain that we aren't certain exactly who the "weak" and "strong" Christians were that Paul was referring to. Some feel the weak were Jewish Christians who followed strict dietary laws, especially on how the animals were slaughtered. To complicate things, some of the choicest cuts of meat in the butcher shops had been offered to idols. Jewish Christians also observed certain days (probably Jewish festivals and the Sabbath) as holier than others. The Jews felt the Gentiles were too liberal, while the Gentiles felt the Jews were too legalistic. No matter what the identity of the groups involved, arguments over matters which were not crucial to salvation obviously threatened the church's unity. Discuss:

☐ *How might the strong become weak by making an issue of food and days?*

☐ *How might the weak become strong by discovering the principle behind the rule?*

☐ *How could each hurt the other by refusing to respect the convictions of the other?*

☐ **Question 13** Suggest that love requires self-limitation for the sake of others. This can mean that selfish people could take over unless Romans 14:19 is practiced. Mutual edification means we don't let others control us because that does not build up the church or the one who controls. Edification means all groups work together to listen to God, to obey God, and to love each other. Invite members to name samples of edifying behavior that maintains personal convictions while building up the body. Ask: **Why is practicing personal convictions secondary to practicing love and unity?**

☐ **Question 14** Suggest that growth in Christ is not always peaceful, but is ultimately peace-producing.